HOW TO
DEAL

MIKE NOVOTNY
and the 922 Ministries Team

Published by Straight Talk Books
P.O. Box 301, Milwaukee, WI 53201
800.661.3311 · timeofgrace.org

Printed in the United States of America
ISBN: 978-1-949488-51-7

Or shame. Because we're not in heaven yet and this is still earth and you and I are still people, we will sin a whole bunch of times in the upcoming year. A few of those sins will feel very shameful. By shameful, I mean they're going to be the kind of sins that you're going to be super afraid to confess. You'll wonder if you still belong in a church, if you can bring up something like "that" to a person like me, or if a person who struggles with something like "those" things could have a place in the family of God. So when that temptation comes and you fall into that sin, how are you going to deal with that?

We're going to cover topics like grief and death, temptation, apathy, and about losing our motivation for seeking God. I hope the things you learn in the chapters to come you don't have to use. I hope you hit your goals without a hitch, but just in case this year is like all the other years, you and I are going to learn how to deal. Because the great news is that there is a God and that God knows all about this year. When that same God inspired the Bible to be written, he wanted to equip you and me for every good work, to be able to walk through our days with more hope and more confidence and more joy and more spiritual tools to fight the good fight and win the race for Jesus.

So let's start in the most important place. Let's *not* start with grief and shame or with anxiety and those people. Let's start with *you*. There's one thing that the future has in common: You. The good days, the bad days, the predictable days, and the crazy days—all the ups and downs include you.

Jesus himself wanted to teach you how to deal with yourself. How to get out of your own head. How to handle the ups and downs in order to end up in a place with more God, more grace, more power, and more blessing. And he does this in the Bible. If you're not very familiar with the Bible,

Jesus actually gave a very simple, succinct, and memorable answer to that question: How do you deal with you?

It's a thing he said right after he got into an argument with his friend Peter. One day, Jesus was explaining to his closest friends, the apostles, about the road he was about to walk. He said, "Guys, we're going to Jerusalem, and when we get there, I'm going to be betrayed. I'm going to be arrested. I'm going to be beaten and mocked and tortured. I'm going to die on a cross, and on the third day, I'm going to rise from the dead." When Jesus' friend Peter heard that, he said, "No. Uh-uh, Jesus." The quote in the Bible (see Matthew 16) is more like this: "Never, Lord! I'm never going to walk down that path, and I will never let you walk down that path either. I will fight. I will defend you. We are not going down that road."

Jesus snapped back fast and said, "Peter, enough! Peter, you are thinking like a man. You're thinking about what's easy right now, what's convenient right now. You're not thinking about the path that leads to the most blessing; you're thinking about the path that is the most convenient to walk in this moment." And Jesus said, "But I'm thinking about you and forgiveness and salvation and reconnection with God. I'm not going to let you stop me from walking that path. Peter, you need to deny that thought, take up your cross, and follow me."

What Jesus had said to Peter wasn't just for Peter, and it wasn't just for the 12 apostles. It's something he wanted every last person on earth to hear. So Jesus stopped his speech and gathered as many possible people as he could and spoke some epic words about how to deal with yourself. In fact, Jesus thought these words were so important that he had them inspired and put down in the Holy Scriptures so you and I could study them.

If you want to know how to deal with you, listen to these incredibly important words from Mark 8:34: **"Then [Jesus] called the crowd to him along with his disciples and said: 'Whoever wants to be my disciple must deny themselves and take up their cross and follow me.'"** "Whoever wants to be my disciple," Jesus said, "must deny themselves." If you want to be a disciple of Jesus. If you want to call yourself a Christian. If you want to follow Jesus down the path to his cross, to Easter morning, and to his empty tomb. If you want to walk with Jesus into the presence of God where you will be forgiven, saved, accepted, and loved for ever and ever, then listen up. Jesus said, "You must deny you."

Jesus said, "You must deny you."

If my Google search is correct, the audio record wasn't invented until the late 1800s. But if it had been around in the first century, I think this is the moment where the soundtrack of Jesus' story would have gone, "Screeeeech." Everyone would have looked up and said, "What did you say, Jesus? You said I have to; I'm required to? There's no other option but to do this? I must deny, reject, pushback, disavow, disassociate? I have to totally separate myself from myself? You're telling me to follow you? I have to deny the world and deny the devil and deny sin to be a Christian, to follow you, and to be a disciple? I have to deny me?" And Jesus said, "Amen!"

If that sounds kind of crazy, it was and it is. Because the number-one message you and I have heard for at least a decade is the exact opposite of that. When was the last time you saw a show or an advertisement marketed at the younger generation that said, "Deny yourself"? We say the exact opposite of that, don't we? We say things like this: "Accept yourself. Be true to yourself. Be yourself. Be true to you. You do you."

The place where I get my hair cut has a little picture up that says, "BeYOUtiful," capital Y-O-U. Be you because you're beautiful! But Jesus was not saying that. He was saying the opposite of that. Think of this: The number-one message my daughters have been raised with, with almost every movie they've ever seen, is anti-Jesus. The air you and I breathe in modern America is anti-Christian because Jesus Christ did not say to be true to you. He said, "I'll tell you how to deal with you: You must deny yourself."

Jesus Christ did not say to be true to you.

Let's push pause quickly and look at exactly what Jesus was saying. Was Jesus saying that everything you feel and think and want and desire and believe is inherently bad? The answer to that question is no. The Bible says when you were created in your mother's womb, God gave you a conscience. That conscience can be twisted and darkened and be off in its calibration, but for a lot of us, our consciences function in some pretty powerful and pretty accurate ways. If you're in a relationship and you want your relationship to be filled with selflessness, that's good. If you desire love and respect or if you have kids and you want your kids to love each other, Jesus was not saying deny that—because your conscience is working correctly.

Here's what Jesus was saying: In this life there are going to be a lot of times when, just like Peter and Jesus in that conversation, the path Jesus is on and the path you'd like to be on are not the same path. There's going to be a whole bunch of times when what you kind of think and what your friends are doing doesn't line up with the path Jesus taught in the Bible. And what Jesus was saying in Mark 8:34 is that if you want to be his disciple, you have to be his disciple. He said that if you want to follow him and you're not following him, then you have to deny yourself and follow him. Jesus was essentially saying, "I have no plans to come to this earth to be your follower, but if you want to follow me, I'd like that. There are going to be times, a lot of times, when you have to deny what you think, change your mind, and agree with what I think."

Let me give you a couple of examples of what this might look like. Let's talk about the people in your life. I bet when it comes to the people in your life—your mom, your dad, your neighbor, the guy you work with, the woman who works in HR, that classmate—I bet in your brain, maybe sometimes, there are two categories of people. There are the people you kind of like and choose to love, and there are the people you kind of don't like, and so you choose not to love, right? They're those folks who really deep in your heart you think, "Listen, they don't deserve my time. They don't deserve my attention after what they said, after the way they behaved, the way they carry themselves, the way they hurt me. Uh-uh, I'm done. They don't deserve it, and no one would blame me." But Jesus wants you to know he is not on that path. Jesus is on the path of crazy, undeserved, unconditional love. God loves the world, and so Jesus said, "Love people. Love the people you like; love the people you don't like. Pray for your enemies. Don't return insult with insult, snark with snark, gossip with gossip. Bless people who don't deserve it. And if you don't agree with that and you want to be my disciple, you have to deny what you think and agree with what I think."

Or how about this example: Sometimes you feel really good at the end of a day because you were really productive; all the little boxes were checked or the to-do list marked off and you said, "Ah!" But what if none of the boxes was checked? To me a good day is a productive day; a day when I don't feel behind or overwhelmed or stressed or like I have to get to work early because there's so much to be done. That's the path I often get on; I rejoice in the days when I get stuff done.

Did you know Jesus does not walk that path? Jesus would quote the Old Testament and say, "No, this is the day God has made. Let's rejoice and be glad in it!" Jesus would say to me, "So, Mike, with your tiny human brain, you came up with a list of eight things you needed to do. But God had only four of them that he wanted done. You did everything God wanted you to do, and now you're mad because you didn't do all eight?" Jesus would say, "No. Walk with me, serve God, and love people, whether your list gets done or not. The good works God had in store for you to do, they are what matters." And Jesus would say to a Type A guy like me, "Mike, you must deny yourself, take up your cross, and follow me."

One last example. How about forgiving yourself? All of us mess up stuff in life; we make choices that we regret. But sometimes we do things that come with enough consequences that we find it almost impossible to forgive ourselves. We feel like it wouldn't be right to truly believe we're loved in this moment, that we're totally forgiven. We think we can't walk around with our heads up as forgiven children of God. And do you know what Jesus would say to that? "I ain't walking that road. Uh-uh, no, no, no. I gave my life on a cross, not so guilt and shame would get the last word but instead so you could wake up every day and know God's mercy is fresh and beautiful and personal with every single breath you take. If you're alive and breathing, praise the Lord. You're forgiven. Pick your head up, child of God, stop dragging your feet, stop thinking you know about forgiveness better than I do. I'm God, and it's finished. You're forgiven."

Do you see how it works? In a thousand different ways—from Type A people to those who beat themselves up for the past—Jesus says that if you don't agree with him and you want to be his disciple, you must deny yourself and follow him. Nothing really matters more for the Christian faith than for a person to say, "Maybe I don't know best; I'm just a person affected very powerfully by my friends, my parents, and my culture. Maybe truth doesn't reside in this heart. Maybe the One who came down from heaven and was called the Way, the Truth, and the Life knows best. Maybe the way to deal with myself is to deny what I think instinctively and to agree with what Jesus thinks."

I can remember one pretty bad experience God let me go through. I was working on one of the biggest projects on my plate; I was getting ready to write a brand-new book and was preparing and working and had invested weeks of time and energy. I had 200 pages of notes and research. I was so jacked up, and I wrote a sample chapter and a book proposal that I was ready to ship off to the publisher. But before I did, I sent it to a couple trusted colleagues for some candid feedback. I sent the email, I went home, and I was all joy. I told my wife, "I cannot wait to sit down and write this book because it will be so good. I'm so excited! It's going to be good for me and good for us, and I hope it's good for the church and for the kingdom." But the next day, my trusted colleagues had replied to my email, and their response was, "Meh."

I had emailed, "Hey, be honest with me. Does this intrigue you to want to read the rest of the book?" One guy said, "Not really." Period. And I would love to tell you that I said, "Thanks for the feedback," but I found myself on a very different road that day. This hasn't happened a lot to me in life, but I kind of lost it. I stared at my computer screen for 30 minutes. I wrote furiously three replies to the people who had given me feedback and, thankfully, deleted them before I sent them. Emotionally, I was in such a terrible spot. I remember I went home at 1:00 in the afternoon and ended my workday right in the middle. If I had a time machine, I would go back right to that moment when the reply ended up in my inbox. I wish I would have said, "Mike, you must deny yourself, because there's a great path that you could walk right now. There's this path that Jesus is on, where Jesus says you did your best, you threw out an idea, and good feedback is going to make it better. **'Wounds from a friend can be trusted,'** the Bible says in Proverbs 27:6, and you can trust what those guys said to you. You don't have to pout; you don't have to cry; you don't have to stare at the screen, because your joy and your happiness isn't in writing books. It's in being loved by God."

I wish I could have gone back and said, "Mike, shut up. Take up your cross, look at yourself in the mirror, say 'you're being stupid,' and get on the path with Jesus because it is a great, great path." I don't have a time machine, but I hope my heart can learn from that experience. What I instinctively feel is not always good or beautiful or right or godly. Sometimes it sabotages my faith and the blessings I could have from taking a step with Jesus.

So how about you? As you think about the path you're on right now and the path Jesus is walking, are there any times that maybe you need to look at yourself in the mirror and say, "No, I know that's what you think and how you feel. I know it's very natural for you to [blank]. But you must deny you and follow him." If that scares you, that's okay. Jesus said taking up a cross and saying no to our hearts sometimes feels like death. But when we walk that path, we find the life that is truly life.

That's why Jesus said this next in Mark 8:35: **"For**

whoever wants to save their life will lose it, but whoever loses their life for me and for the gospel will save it." I love those words. This very quote sent me down the path to becoming a pastor. I thought of all the people who were doing their thing and being true to themselves and following their hopes and dreams and resolutions, who were going to lose life with God, and I said to myself, "I have

But when we walk that path, we find the life that is truly life.

to come up with some way, whatever I can do, to get people off this path and on to Jesus' path." I wanted to convince them that being true to yourself might be comfortable and easy and convenient in the moment, but there is something infinitely better, a life that can be found with Jesus. He says if you give up being true to yourself, you will save your life and will go through every day for the rest of your life with God at your side.

I honestly don't know of anything better that I could possibly say to you. The difficult part of being a Christian is that Jesus gets to be the King and the Lord, and he gets the last word. But the beautiful part about being a Christian is that every day you get to live with God. The good days and the bad days, you're not alone in the kingdom of God because there is a King and he's God. You get to go through the highs and the lows, the tragedies and the celebrations, with a Father who knows you and loves you, who's not ashamed to be with you, who uses all his compassion to take care of you. And you get to walk with Jesus, the Savior who went to a cross, who gave up his own life, who walked the narrow road of pain so you can be forgiven and adored by a Father in heaven every single day—your good moral days and the days you fall on your face. You get up and there's Jesus and more grace and more love. You get to walk every day with the Holy

Spirit, the Spirit who says, "Yes, you can. You can forgive. I'm going to get you through this. No, anxiety isn't going to get the last word over you. Yes, I know this is difficult, but I'm going to keep you strong."

That is the road I want to be on, don't you! I have no clue what's coming this year, but if I'm walking a path with the Father and the Son and the Spirit at my side, I'm going to be okay. So will you. Lose that old life, embrace this new one, and throughout this year, I want you to ask just one question: Does Jesus agree with me?

I wish I could have asked that question as I was sitting at my computer after reading my colleagues thoughts about my book idea: "Does Jesus agree with me? Is Jesus throwing an emotional tantrum right now? No? Okay, then you must deny yourself and follow him. You can't forgive yourself; I get it. Does Jesus agree with that? No." *Does Jesus agree with me* is the simple question to teach you how to deal with you.

Let me give you 365 days' worth of homework. I want you to pray the Lord's Prayer every day. If you're not familiar with the Lord's Prayer, here are the words:

Our Father in heaven, hallowed be your name, your kingdom come, your will be done on earth as in heaven. Give us today our daily bread. Forgive us our sins as we forgive those who sin against us. Lead us not into temptation, but deliver us from evil. For the kingdom, the power, and the glory are yours now and forever. Amen.

Remember, this is the classic prayer that Jesus taught, and it's a reminder of who you and I are. We're the children of God through faith in Jesus Christ. It's a bold prayer that says, "God, forgive me for everything. Don't lead me into the temptation of following the path that's natural. Deliver me from that kind of evil thinking."

But what I see in this prayer is again and again a desire to agree with Jesus. We pray: "Not my name, Jesus, hallowed be your name. Not my kingdom come, Jesus, but yours. Not my will be done, Jesus, but yours. Not mine is the power and the kingdom and the glory; it's not about me. It's about you, and I want to follow you every step of the way." If you pray this, day after day after day, if you slow down just a little bit and meditate on its

I want to follow you every step of the way.

words, then you'll know exactly how to deal with yourself. You'll know who you are—a child of God, forgiven through the blood of Christ—and you'll know what life is about—his kingdom, his will, and his glory.

I invite you to close your eyes and take a deep breath. Before you begin this prayer, I want you to envision the smiling, beaming, proud face of your Father in heaven. It is to that amazing God we pray. He is the Father whom Jesus is leading us to. Now pray the words of the Lord's Prayer.

Does Jesus agree with you? If you pray that prayer with God's will in mind, he always will.

Points to Ponder

Gather—Read Hebrews 13:7,8: **"Remember your leaders, who spoke the word of God to you. Consider the outcome of their way of life and imitate their faith. Jesus Christ is the same yesterday and today and forever."** Consider why Jesus wants every Christian to be a part of a spiritual community with organized leadership.

Group—Benjamin Franklin once said that one of the hardest things in life is to know yourself. Why would that be? How does doing life together with other Christians help you follow Jesus faithfully?

Grow—You were challenged at the end of this chapter to pray the Lord's Prayer every day for the next year. To start off strong, mark this new habit in your calendar or on a sticky note on your bathroom mirror.

Give—As you consider your financial goals, take some time to pray and ask God about how you could become a more generous giver. Then take a bold next step, trusting God always cares for his children.

Go—Share this message with a friend who might be searching for a better "life."

Prayer—Jesus, when you challenge me and command me to change, when you tell me to deny myself and take up a cross, there's no doubt it will be painful. But help me believe you are on the other side of that cross. No matter what it costs me, I'll give it up because you are worth it. I pray all these things, Jesus, in your powerful and saving name. Amen.

Chapter 2

How to Deal With People

According to a 2013 story from the *New York Times*, the average American knows about 600 people. That means if you put together your family and your extended family, your friends and your acquaintances, your roommates, your neighbors, your classmates, your cousins, your second cousins, and the people you kind of recognize, the average person knows about 600 people.

I love thinking about that number because I've learned in life what many have: People have potential. You don't need 1,000 people to change your life. You don't even need 600 people. You don't need 60 people. You don't even need 6 people. Sometimes it's just 1 or 2 or a very small group of people who influence us in profound ways.

As you look back on your life story, can you think of just one person who made a tremendous impact in your life? One person you kind of knew but then you got close, and the impact was visible? Just one friend, just one teacher, just one guy you ran into at church, and he asked you out for coffee. And now you have three kids together. I love thinking about the sheer potential of people. If that number is true, in my next season of life God might use just a few to bring me closer to his Son, Jesus. And the exact same thing is true for you. In the next month, the next year, the next decade, a few of those people could bring you closer to Jesus than ever before.

God could use that one young woman in your class to teach you how to deal with anxiety. You've been losing that battle for too long, and God's going to use her—her experience and her wisdom—to help you.

Or maybe you've been struggling to get sober, and God's going to use that one guy. It's going to be one conversation, which turns into one big ask, one mentorship, one sponsor, a first day, and then a next day of sobriety—just one person.

It's going to be that person whom you meet at college or in the neighborhood after you move or in the nursing home. Someone who shows you kindness and love, someone who prays for you and encourages you, that person who just nudges you day after day in the direction of Jesus.

Or, if I can be real with you, it might be one person who does the opposite. If you ask an addict about their story, it often goes back to one person. One person who invited them out for a drink. One person who offered them a drug for the first time. One person who brought them to a party where they were introduced to their future dealer. It only takes one person. It only takes a few people whom you meet when

People can lead you in one of two directions.

you're in middle school or high school to lead you down a path that your mother was worried about. It doesn't take a thousand, doesn't even take 600, just 1. You see, people have potential. That's true no matter how old you are, male or female, churchgoing or not; people can lead you in one of two directions. And that's why I want to ask a big question: How do you deal with people? If you're an average American and God's going to put 600 people into your life in this next year, how do you deal with them?

I have to admit, in the past my answer to that question has been pretty good, but not *really good*. My answer for how to treat people in your family, at work, at church often comes down to these two words: *You first.* Love people; put them first. Put their wants before your needs. Be selfless and sacrificial like Jesus; that's how we're blessed and how we thrive. But I've learned that's not always good advice. And I learned that from the wisest man in the ancient world. King Solomon was the third king of Israel. He was known as this man of great wisdom, and he wrote this in the Bible: **"The righteous choose their friends carefully"** (Proverbs 12:26). He didn't say righteous people, people who are right with God and want to do the right thing, you just treat everyone the same. No, he said the righteous choose their friends carefully. That's what a good dad would say to his beloved daughter, right? Be careful; love people. Be selfless, but treat people differently; don't hang out with just anyone. This is great wisdom: "The righteous choose their friends carefully."

That's what I want to address. Obviously I can't write out 600 different scenarios, so I want to break the people you know down into three groups: red-light people, green-light people, and yellow-light people. Let's look at King Solomon's words in Proverbs and see a wise way to treat each group of people.

Let's start with red-light people. If you drive, you know that *red* means "stop." Did you know that God himself says some of the relationships in your life need to stop? People you're hanging out with, people you're texting with, people you're partying with, God says, "I want you to stop, U-turn, hit the gas, and get away." Now that might not seem very Christian, right? But it is very Christian. In fact, let me prove it to you. Proverbs 14:7 says, **"Stay away from a fool."** Read that again: "Stay away from a fool." God says that to you! You should love all people like God loves all people. You can pray for all people, but sometimes you have to pray while you stay away.

But what does God mean by a "fool"? Are fools people who sin? Because we all sin. Are fools people who struggle with sin and go back to old habits? Because all of us do that in one way or another. Who exactly are you and I supposed to stay away from? I tried to find the answer to that question in the book of Proverbs. A few weeks ago, I read the book of Proverbs, all 31 chapters from start to finish, to look specifically for who qualifies as a fool. Here's what I learned: Foolish people often do foolish things. They're angry people; they run their tongues; they drink too much; etc. But it really wasn't the actions that a person did but the attitude behind those actions that qualified them as a fool. If I could summarize a fool's attitude in one word, the word would be *whatever*. You know someone in your life is a fool when they're doing something that's bad and their reaction is, "Whatever."

Maybe your husband's working too much. Maybe your wife is overcommitted and stressed and there are issues. A foolish spouse would say, "Whatever, it's fine."

Or maybe you're dating someone. There are some red flags—the way he gets so tense, even angry, maybe even violent when he's frustrated—and you say, "Maybe we should talk to someone. Maybe we should go see the pastor. Maybe we should schedule a visit with a counselor." And if he's a fool, he'll say, "Whatever."

Maybe you have some friends, and you're concerned that going out for a drink has turned into something more for them. It's compulsive. It's a habit. It's an addiction. And you want to talk, saying, "I don't think this is normal." "Whatever," they say.

Someone who's "whatevering" their sin—where God says, "This is not okay. This is not fine," and they say, "It's fine. It's okay. Don't worry about it. Stop bringing it up"—is a red-light person. God says, as much as you can, depending on the relationship status, if this is your roommate, your friend, your neighbor, your teammate, stay away from a fool.

And here's why. It might seem a little bit like tough love, like kind of unchristian and unkind, but the Bible says this: **"A companion of fools suffers harm"** (Proverbs 13:20). The passage doesn't say that if you're a companion of fools you'll turn into a fool. No, you might not; you might have the self-control to stay away from their sins, but it does promise this: A companion of fools suffers harm.

My childhood pastor described it like this: Take a Ziplock bag and put six pieces of dusty coal inside. Imagine for a second that these are six foolish people at your school or in your circle of friends. What do you think would happen if I open the Ziplock bag and drop you in (a marshmallow)? What's going to happen? Will the marshmallow automatically turn into a piece of coal? No. But you can guess what will happen. Zip it up, let these people hang out with each other, spend too much time, and the dust rubs off.

My childhood pastor used to say, "Show me your friends, and I'll show you your future." You might not become them, but you will become affected by them. In this Proverbs passage, our heavenly Father says the exact same thing. He's a good Dad, and he says, "Watch out. A companion of fools suffers harm."

Are you thinking about anyone right now? Is there a friend you've been making excuses for too long? Have you gotten caught up in the drama too many times? She's a gossip and you're too close, so people lump you in with her? He has an anger problem, but he's your teammate and you've been excusing it. You find yourself in the middle of the arguments, the fights, and all the drama. It's not fun to play on the team anymore. Our heavenly Father in love says what I would say to my own kids: Stay away from a fool, because a companion of fools suffers harm. The righteous choose their friends carefully.

If you want to change, if you want life to be different, you need people because the righteous choose their friends carefully. So choose people carefully. If you know a fool in your life (a red-light person), stay away because a companion of fools suffers harm.

I'm going to swing all the way over now and talk about green-light people. I probably don't have to tell you the word *green*, the color green, means "go." Go for it. Don't smash the brakes; don't tap the brakes. You hit the gas and invest as much time and energy into those people as you can. Here's a great Bible passage to prove it. Proverbs 13:20 says, **"Walk with the wise and become wise."** When you walk with wise people, you become a wise person.

When you walk with wise people, you become a wise person.

If those chunks of coal and that marshmallow weren't foolishness but wisdom, the same thing would happen to you. The closer you get to people like that, the more their wisdom rubs off on you.

Think for a second what that passage must have meant three thousand years ago. There was no texting, no direct messaging, no Facebook chats, no FaceTime, no Zoom. If you wanted to walk with wise people, you literally had to walk with wise people. You had to be in their presence, and that is the supercharged way to become wise, to be with people.

Do you know anyone who's wise? As you think about that big circle of 600 people you kind of know, is there anyone whose life or faith or family, whose parenting, whose character is different, better, not average? Maybe you have a friend who has been through agonizing cancer. She was sick like so often cancer patients are, and yet through the midst of it, she did not take her eyes off Jesus. And when you spoke with her, faith just came out of her: Scripture, promises, and truth. That is a wise person.

Do you have a friend who gives away money, lots of it, and he seems really happy about it? When everyone else is trying to save and invest and go on their trips, he's giving to the poor, giving to ministry, spreading the name of Jesus. He doesn't seem sad. What is it that makes him that way? He's a wise person. Have you ever seen a married couple who's been together for many years yet he still holds her hand? In a world where it's so easy to poke fun at the other gender, she doesn't scoff at her husband but respects him, builds him up, makes him feel bigger. Those are some wise people.

I'm sure if you stop and think, if you let the Holy Spirit bring some names into your heart and mind, you will know the people whom God wants you to walk with. And once those names come to mind, here's the command of your loving Father: "Walk with the wise and become wise."

I warn you, this will not necessarily be easy. There's kind of a famous book that came out a few years ago from an Australian author named Bronnie Ware. She wrote about her experiences in speaking with dying people in palliative care. In particular, Bronnie asked them if they had any regrets. She was speaking to these people during the last days of their lives, and do you know what the dying people told her? They told her they regretted not walking with the wise. Bronnie said this: "They told me I wish I would have stayed in touch with my friends." In the busyness of life and work and career and moving, people always say, "You know, we should get together. We should do this more often," but they don't, and the busyness of life just sweeps them away. So I want to encourage you to learn from their example.

Here's my simple advice to you: Schedule your steps. If you know a wise person and they're open to a relationship like that, schedule it. Maybe this is my Type A trying to impose on you, but I think if you get it on a calendar—every first Saturday of the month for breakfast or every Friday after we drop the kids off at school or once a quarter—it prioritizes it, protects it, because God has given us this great promise: The one who walks with the wise will grow wise. I want to encourage you to do the same.

Which means we're down to one last category. Red-light people: stay away from a fool. Green-light people: walk with the wise. And that brings us to yellow-light people. Technically a yellow light is not for hitting the gas. The official governmental recommendation is that a yellow light means "slow down and proceed with caution." And that's a really good way to think about most of the 600 people you know. They're probably not notably wise. You probably don't know that much yet, and I'm hoping and guessing that most of them aren't fools either, those who say, "Whatever." Most of them are kind of in the middle. So what should you do? Here's what King Solomon says. He writes in Proverbs 2:4: **"Look for [wisdom] as for silver and search for it as for hidden treasure."** I love those verbs. *Look* for it. *Search* for it. Finding a wise person is like a hidden treasure; it's more valuable than silver, so keep your eyes open and search. And here's the part I love: Because if you do, you might find them.

Keep your eyes open and search.

I was thinking of my own story the other day. The people I am closest to today, the people I reach out to when I need prayer, the people I unload my burdens on and confess my sins to, the people I can send a 911 text to ("I'm not in a good spot; I need you right now"), the people who bring me back to the cross of Jesus Christ—most of them I didn't even know ten years ago. But then I moved to a new city, I came to a new church, and these strangers walked through the door.

At first they were just faces and then kind of acquaintances and then I kind of knew them from Bible study. Then they became friends and then great friends. I love thinking about that. There was this treasure of a relationship, and I had to look for it and search for it and grasp and hold on to it. And the same thing is true for you. That's a crazy thought! Sitting with you in church next week might be your future best friends. Working right next to you in the hospital or in accounting or in the factory might be the future mother of your children. The person you kind of know and maybe remember their name at work or in your neighborhood, they could become that person, and so God says be wise, open your eyes, look and search for wisdom as for hidden treasure.

There's a guy at our church who had heard me talking about community who asked me, "How do I find my people?" He was wondering how to find people to do life with. He wanted relationships like the one I just described where you can confess and forgive and pray and be real, and he didn't have that just yet. So he asked me, "Pastor, what do I do? Do I just keep coming to church, and then it just happens? Do I go to a Bible study or a life group and sooner or later I'll end up with it?"

I told him there are no guarantees. Relationships are relationships, and people are people. But here's what I have seen as the secret recipe of getting community: Be real. In my experience, you can go to a church and can have brothers and sisters and cousins; you can have coworkers, a roommate, a small group, a Bible study, but those will never become great relationships until you get real. And so I encouraged him, "Go back to church, go back to group, swallow hard, swallow your pride, and be real."

Confess what you're struggling with. Admit vulnerably a sin that you've committed, and then look. Because in moments like that, wise people take a step forward. They say, "Me too." They encourage, "I'll pray for you." They might not say anything in the moment, but a day later or further on in that week, they'll text you: "Hey, I've been thinking about you. How are you doing?" And wise people, selfless people with strong character, will step forward. You will know exactly whom to walk with. The Bible says don't speed through life like it's all a green light; slow down. Proceed with caution. Open your eyes and ears, confess, be real, and search because you might just find a hidden treasure.

When you put that all together, you've got God's wisdom on how to deal with people. Stay away from fools, walk with the wise, slow down, and search.

As I was thinking about these three categories of people and writing about them, I started to wonder what Jesus would think as he looked at me. Would he want to be with me? Would Jesus stay away from me? I didn't like thinking about that. I try not to be a fool, but I honestly can think about times when someone criticized me and my reaction was, "Whatever; it's fine." I can think of times when I could have been a wise person and could have been better, but I gave in to sinful ways. It made me ask the question: What would Jesus think of me? If Jesus, who is the wisdom of God, wants to deal with people in God's way, how would he deal with me?

But then I remembered what I had read. Before the thought that Jesus was out the door, U-turning, taking off from my life and yours, I read this passage from the book of Proverbs: **"There is a friend who sticks closer than a brother"** (18:24). There is a friend; a friend who's even better than flesh and blood. There is a friend who sticks with you even better than your own family. There's a friend who does not bail on you even when you deserve it.

There is a friend just like that. His name is Jesus. Jesus is wiser than Solomon. He is the very wisdom of God and yet, what did Jesus do? He could have stayed away from all the foolishness and brokenness and hurtfulness of this planet, but in love he did not. Instead, he came and walked with us. Not because you and I are so wise but because he is so good. Jesus knew the passage. He was one with the Holy Spirit who inspired these words: **"A companion of fools suffers harm"** (Proverbs 13:20). But Jesus, in shocking love, was willing to be harmed. He walked with Judas, with Peter, with James and John, with sinners. And he walks with us too. He walked all the way to

Through faith, Jesus sticks with you.

a cross. He was willing to be ruined so we could walk with God forever. There's an old hymn that says, "What a friend we have in Jesus." And isn't that true? Jesus sticks with us.

You might have some great people in your life or not. But through faith, Jesus sticks with you. You might have a great group of people to do life with that you could be totally transparent with or maybe you don't, not yet, but you can with Jesus. Before he ascended into heaven, Jesus gave his disciples a great mission, and then he gave them a great promise: **"Surely I am with you always"** (Matthew 28:20).

I'll admit, 600 people—that's complicated. It's difficult to know what's the wise thing to do, but you have a firm foundation. You have Jesus. That Jesus will never leave you, never forsake you. He will always walk by your side. The Lord is my Shepherd. He guides me; he leads me. His mercy and goodness are following me. I have Jesus, so I know how to deal. You have him too. With his help, you'll always know how to deal with people.

Points to Ponder

Gather—Could a red-light person be a member of a local church? If so, how? If that seems unlikely, why would being part of a church family be a great way to become wiser? Read Hebrews 10:23-25 for a few of God's answers: **"Let us hold unswervingly to the hope we profess, for he who promised is faithful. And let us consider how we may spur one another on toward love and good deeds, not giving up meeting together, as some are in the habit of doing, but encouraging one another—and all the more as you see the Day approaching."**

Group—Evaluate the following statement: Being in a small group with other Christians is a way to grow in wisdom.

Grow—Would you like to grow in wisdom regarding racial diversity? Check out voiceofthemiddleground.com for resources and events.

Give—Meditate on these two classic passages on dealing with money. Jot down at least three insights, and then pray God would make you wise with every dollar he gives you.

Proverbs 3:9,10: **"Honor the Lᴏʀᴅ with your wealth, with the firstfruits of all your crops; then your barns will be filled to overflowing, and your vats will brim over with new wine."**

Proverbs 23:4,5: **"Do not wear yourself out to get rich; do not trust your own cleverness. Cast but a glance at riches, and they are gone, for they will surely sprout wings and fly off to the sky like an eagle."**

Go—Do you know anyone who struggles with worry and fear? Share this resource with them.

Prayer—Dear Father, this matters. So please help me. Give me wisdom and the courage to do what I have to do in my relationships. I want to thrive and grow and become wise as I walk with Jesus, so please help me. Help me deal with people just like Jesus did with love, compassion, patience, and grace. I pray this all in his beautiful name. Amen.

Chapter 3
How to Deal With Anxiety

Not too long ago, I had my first real, personal encounter with anxiety. For most of my life, I've been kind of a logical, rational, biblical kind of guy, so I had never seen anxiety face-to-face until then.

I was working with a vocal coach in Milwaukee. I was standing in his living room. He was a great, encouraging guy. I personally signed up for the lesson because I wanted to work on some bad habits with my voice. And as he was talking through this and that and let's try this and tweak that or let's try that one more time, I suddenly, for some inexplicable reason, could feel both my body and my brain starting to unravel. I noticed my breath was getting shallow and my hands were starting to sweat. At one point, it dawned on me that my toes were curled up in my shoes and standing vertically. He asked me for one of the exercises to practice being loud and then to whisper, but my body and my neck were so tense that I found it impossible, physically impossible, to whisper.

The guy—who I know pretty well—said, "Are you okay?"

I couldn't come up with an answer. I just told him, "I'm sorry. I've got to leave." And so I did. My wife picked me up at his house, and I got into the car.

She wondered why the lesson was done early and said, "What happened?"

I said, "I don't know." It's hard to explain the physical reaction I had that day, and I cannot give you a logical or reasonable explanation. But I can guarantee you this: It was incredibly emotional and insanely powerful.

That's how anxiety works. According to the National Alliance of Mental Illness, anxiety like that is the number-one mental health struggle in America. Twenty percent of American adults, one in five grown-ups, deals with experiences like this almost every day. And if you've read the stories, you know that scientists and psychologists are still trying to figure out why among children and teenagers, especially girls, anxiety seems to be skyrocketing at unprecedented levels.

Maybe you know exactly what that's like, because one in five means that most families or extended families deal with chronic general anxiety. Now, anxiety, by that definition, is not just the nerves you feel before a first date or a big test or a presentation at work. Anxiety is when you get stuck in a "what-if" question. What if this happens to me? And what if that happens to me? And what about this and what about that? Where most people would quickly engage their reason, logic, and experience to deal with that thought, people who struggle with anxiety can't.

Let me describe it this way. For most of us, worrisome thoughts are like a snowflake that falls on the warm cement of logic. But for people who regularly battle anxiety, that one little what-if question doesn't melt; it quickly snowballs. And one question leads to another, and soon it snowballs into this avalanche of a worst-case scenario. The worst possible thing is going to happen, and it's going to happen to me. I'm going to beat all the odds, and my life is about to fall apart; that's anxiety.

Or to put it another way. Anxiety is like a one-loop roller coaster. For most of us we go through life like a roller coaster; there are ups and downs, there are fun parts, and there are scary loops that we go through but then get out of them. But the people whom you know and love who struggle with anxiety get stuck in the loop. There's a scary thought, and then they think about the scary thought again. They stay up at night, and they think about the scary thought again. It turns their stomach, and they stare at the ceiling and can't sleep. That's anxiety. And 20 percent of the people we know and love and maybe you live with have a condition just like that.

In fact, if you're a Christian, you might live with a condition that's actually worse than that, because anxiety happens among Christians too. Some people think it happens in really unique and even more powerful ways because while a non-Christian might worry about their finances and their friends and their family and their tests and their health and everything else, Christians often worry about their own Christianity. Most of us know the Bible says we should trust God and not worry, but when we don't do that and we do this, we feel even more anxious. I could easily name people who pray to Jesus every day, who open their Bibles on a daily basis, and who constantly wonder if they're even going to make it to heaven. They get stuck in this

Does God love me?

looping thought: "Well, I'm still worried, and worrying is a sin that means my faith is weak. Maybe I'm not sorry for that sin, and maybe I'm not really worthy. Maybe God really is angry," and they get stuck in that thought. After all these years, they still wonder the most basic question in the world: Does God love me? Am I right with him? Am I going to make it?

My question for you is this: How do you deal with anxiety? If anxiety's what you're living with, how do you deal? If the girl you're dating or the guy you're married to or the kid you're raising or your roommate at college or a friend from church or your mom or your dad has anxiety, how do you deal?

I've got to be honest with you that about five years ago,

I had no clue how to deal with anxiety. I was too logical and black and white. I was too simplistic. I used to say things like, "Well, that's not going to happen!" And then I'd grab my Bible, and I'd open to the passage that says, "Don't worry." I'd read it and say, "There! You're welcome. Shall we pray?" By the grace of God, some challenges have come into my life that have allowed me to be much wiser. So I want to share with you what I've learned from not just experience but from the Word itself and from others. In the Bible, I found out there are 30 different passages that use the words *worry*, *worried*, *anxious*, or *anxiety*, and I want to share a bunch of them with you. As I do so, I want to share with you a bunch of stories of brothers and sisters who I believe have strong faith but deal with anxious thoughts all the time, and I want to share with you how they deal so you and I can deal with anxiety better than ever before.

Now as powerful as I hope this chapter will be, it's not going to fix it. Because that's not how it works. If I was writing about pride or jealousy, you wouldn't think, "Oh yeah, I used to be proud. Then I read this book that one time, and now it's better." No, you're wise enough to know your spiritual life is a journey and humility and trust are like fruit that grow on a tree. Sometimes it takes time. So my expectation is that I'm going to give you a bunch of seeds that I hope you can plant and think about and water and fertilize. Maybe not today or even this year but in time the Holy Spirit will produce the fruit of love and of peace in your heart so the next time those intrusive thoughts come, you can escape them with the help and the promises of God.

I'm going to cover four things. The first thing you should do to deal with anxiety is breathe. Now you might think I'm a heretic for this next part, but I actually think that before you open your Bible, you should breathe. Here's why: Have you ever seen a two-year-old who is about three hours past his last nap? He's freaking out, he's crabby, and he's punching Mom and talking back to Dad. When that kid is being disrespectful and selfish, do you say, "Well, son, we're going to bring you to church so you can hear the Word of God about crabbiness." No, what do you do with the kid? You give him a nap, right?

Have you ever been hangry before? When you're hangry, do you really need 15 different Bible passages on anger? What you probably need is a sandwich. There's a way to deal with that anger, right? So with the kid and with your own hunger, we know that there's a connection between our physical bodies and our spiritual lives; the same is true with anxiety. It's very tempting to jump in and find the first Bible passage on anxiety, but there actually is a physical connection to the anxiousness that you feel.

I learned something fascinating the other day. Did you know right in the middle of your head is a little almond-shaped thing called the amygdala? You remember that from science class? The amygdala is responsible—one of many things—for the fight or flight reaction of your body. If you were suddenly in danger—let's just say an actual lion came up to you and roared—your amygdala would kick in. Here's what it would do: It would use your nervous system to say, "All systems: Survival!" And it would start reallocating blood from your prefrontal cortex, which is the thinking part of your brain, and sending it to your muscles so you can fight the lion. It would take blood and energy from your digestive system, because you don't need to digest your breakfast if you're about to be digested, and it would send it to your legs so you could take flight and survive, right? Your amygdala is this brilliant way of keeping you safe from danger.

But your amygdala is famous for false alarms. It goes off

and triggers that same reaction in your body, even if there's not a lion near you. Even if you're not actually in danger. Even if there's no one evil in your bedroom at night. Just the thought of it causes your body to have a physical reaction. That's what happened to me that day with my vocal coach. What happens is sometimes you feel sick when you're anxious, right? Your blood and energy have been taken out of this system to help you survive. And if I jump too quickly and open my Bible and say, "Let's think about the promises of God! Let's think logically about this situation that you're in," guess what your brain in that moment is least likely to do? Think.

What's the answer? Breathe. Scientists have found that you can actually use your nervous system in reverse. When you take a bunch of deep breaths, it sends a message back to your amygdala: "You're okay." If I was running from a lion right now, I'd be breathing pretty hard and fast. **What's the answer? Breathe.** But the fact that I can breathe slowly and I'm not in danger sends blood back up to my brain so I can think. That's how you deal.

I read a great book last year about anxiety in young girls, and the author compared it to a glitter jar. It contains glitter, water, glue, and a tight cap, of course. When you have an anxious thought, when you're worried about politics or your own health or getting sick or traveling or flying in a plane, what you see when you shake the glitter jar is what happens inside of your head, inside of your heart, inside of your body. Everything's swirling around so fast. If I try to preach to you and teach you a Bible passage in this moment, you're too frazzled. So here's what you need to do: You need to calm your glitter. One counselor actually keeps one of these on her desk. When someone comes in and wants to pour out their problems, she shakes it up and says, "Let's just wait." And they breathe for a few minutes until the glitter calms down and the person is ready to talk and think and deal with anxiety.

If that's you, here's the first place to start: Breathe.

Once you're ready to think, what do you do next? Here's number two: You pray. There are 30 passages in the Bible that deal with worry and anxiety. A bunch of them were written by the apostles Paul and Peter, and they both agree on this: When you feel anxious, you should pray. Here's what the apostle Paul said in Philippians 4:6: **"Do not be anxious about anything, but in every situation, by prayer and petition, with thanksgiving, present your requests to God."** And then Peter thought that was pretty smart, so he gave his own version in 1 Peter 5:7: **"Cast all your anxiety on [God] because he cares for you."** I love that! I love how all-inclusive those passages are. God doesn't say, "Listen, I'm God. I'm kind of a big deal. I've got a lot to handle. A lot of people pray to me, so if it's something really big, then you can talk to me about it." No. Did you catch the passages? Cast *all, all of it.* If you told your best friend about everything you worried about, she would want some space from you. But God never needs space. He is a Father of bottomless compassion. You never run out of minutes in your conversation and connection with God. There's not a single thing, no matter how big or how small, how logical or how crazy, that your Father in heaven will roll his eyes at. He says, "Come to me. You're my kid. I don't want you to live like this. I don't want you to be afraid. Cast it on me. Tell me what you want. Tell me how I can help. I don't want you to be anxious about anything, so cast everything on me."

That's what one sister in the faith does. There's a woman

who's been coming to our church for a few years who has always struck me as an incredibly strong Christian. I know she's been through a lot in her life, and yet she is without shaken faith but closer to God than ever before. A couple of weeks ago though, we were in the church lobby. I over-heard her mention that for her entire life she's had to deal with anxiety. So as I was preparing to write about anxiety, I reached out to her and I said, "How do you deal?" She said I could share her story with you.

Her anxiety started, tragically, young because her father was not a good man. He was abusive, and he was dangerous. So as a very little girl she had to learn how to deal. She was always in fight-or-flight mode, always cognizant of what kind of mood her father was in, not wanting to set him off. But as she got older and separated herself from that danger, she realized not everyone was dangerous; she didn't always have to live in panic mode, so she needed to figure out how to fight those intrusive thoughts.

I asked her, "How do you do it?" This is what she said:

"How do I deal? I don't. I don't handle anxiety because I can't handle anxiety. It is only through Christ that victory is found." I love that line! I picture this woman desperately praying, "God, I can't. I can't make myself stop thinking about something. How do you even do that? But you can. Help."

It is only through Christ that victory is found.

I want to encourage you to pray. For some of you, in your clear, non-anxious moments, maybe you write out a simple 911 prayer: "God, help." Maybe you write down this passage: "Cast all your anxiety on him." Maybe you put a couple of note cards by your bed or in your Bible so when your brain isn't working well, you can run to the Word and say, "But God cares, and God wants to help. I don't just have to breathe and use some physical technique; there's a spiritual power that I can tap into, and so I pray."

And then the third way to deal with anxiety: You seek. From cover to cover in the Bible, there are 30 passages on worry and anxiety, but 8 of them are found in the exact same spot. You might know the famous words that Jesus spoke in the Sermon on the Mount about worry. He was talking about the birds of the air and the flowers of the field and if God takes care of these things that don't have a soul, how much more will he take care of his kids who do? And in that teaching in Matthew chapter 6, Jesus spoke these words: **"Do not worry about your life"** (verse 25). Pretty all-inclusive, huh? Here's what you should do: **"But seek first his kingdom and his righteousness"** (verse 33). If you're feeling anxious, if someone you love is feeling anxious, you should pray and then seek God. You should go after God as your refuge. You should think about God's promises and blessings as much as you can and seek the safety of his kingdom. Talk to each other about the kingdom of God and the righteousness of God.

Now if you're new to the Bible, that might not mean much to you, but it is beautiful. Here's why. The kingdom of God is the place where God is the King. Picture an ancient city like Jerusalem with big, high walls that you couldn't get past and gates and bars and towers and guards. Inside that kingdom, God is the King, and he rules with authority and uses his authority for your safety. If you believe in Jesus, by the grace of God, you are part of the kingdom of God. That means that King Jesus is going to keep you safe. The devil is a roaring lion, and he can prowl around outside the walls and roar and lie and accuse you and ask you, "What if this?" and, "What if that?" The one thing he can't do is get through the gates that are barred with the blood of Jesus Christ. He cannot get you. That's his kingdom. I know many

Christians who think, "What if I don't make it? And what if my faith isn't strong enough? And what if my worry and my sin are too much? And what if I lose my salvation?" Seek the kingdom because King Jesus isn't going to let you go. And if you're worried about your salvation—if you're panicking because you think your faith is too small—let me preach at you. This next part is not a suggestion; it's preaching. This is not my opinion, my word; this is the Word of your King Jesus. He said, "I'm your Shepherd. You're my sheep. And no one will snatch you out of my hands."

No one. In Romans chapter 8, the Bible says, "There is nothing, not life, death, not angels, not demons, not the present or the future; there is nothing in all creation that can separate you from the love of God that is in Christ Jesus."

Nothing. In Philippians 1:6, the apostle Paul said this: **"He who began a good work in you will carry it on to completion."** He's going to finish it. He's going to get you to the finish line. He will get you to heaven. Do you know what the word *will* means? It means "will." And one last time, if you didn't get my point just yet, the Bible says that if you're a Christian, God put the Holy Spirit into your heart as a deposit guaranteeing what is to come. You want to guess what the word *guarantee* means? It means you're going to be okay. I know you don't believe that, and I know you don't think that, but you're going to be okay. The devil can lie to you, and he can accuse you that you're not good enough. He can roar, but you are inside the kingdom. King Jesus ain't letting you out. That's his righteousness. By the blood of Jesus, you have been made right with God.

In fact, Philippians 1:6 should become your next tattoo. And I think your next tattoo after that, based off of Matthew 6:33, should be just one word: *His.* Do you love the possessive pronoun as much as I do?

I'll take you all the way back to third grade. Do you remember the possessive pronouns? *My, yours, theirs, his*—did you catch that in Matthew 6:33? What should you seek? What should you think about when you're anxious? His righteousness. If it said, "Seek your righteousness," you'd have to constantly think: "Am I doing the right thing? Am I living the right life? Am I good enough for God? Am I right with God?" But it doesn't say that; it says *his*. I'm thinking about how Jesus did the right thing, how he was righteous. How at the cross when he bled and died for me, on Easter morning when he rose from the grave for me, he—singlehandedly—made me right with the Father. And when you're anxious, these are the things that you seek.

That's what one brother in the faith told me to tell you. I know a guy who loves Jesus and worries about his faith all the time. He's actually a guy who sometimes gets to teach the Bible and tell people that they're saved. About once a month he emails me and asks me if he's saved. And I've known him long enough and loved him long enough that I always know what to say to him: "Let's stop talking about you; let's talk about Jesus." I emailed him before writing this and said, "Hey, I'm going to write to people about anxiety. What should I write?" And here's what he told me: "Mike, make sure they know that Jesus loves them even when they're not trusting Jesus like they should." So let me take his advice and remind you that you're loved, not because you're a great person, not because you trust as much as you should. Jesus loves you because he does.

Stop talking about you. Let's talk about Jesus.

That's why my favorite anxiety passage is Psalm 94:18,19. It says this: **"When I said, 'My foot is slipping,' your unfailing love, Lord, supported me. When anxiety was great**

within me, your consolation brought me joy." Maybe you should add to your tattoo, not just a "his" but a "your." When anxiety was *great within me*—not *after* I cured my anxiety. In the moment that it happened, God, your consolation, your unfailing love, supported and brought you joy. Seek the promises of God, the love of God, and you'll know how to deal.

So first, exhale. Second, pray. Third, seek. And now, finally, don't just bring God into it, bring other people into the battle. There's a woman from our church who's dealt with anxiety for a long time. In fact, she leads the life group that we have at our church to help people with anxiety and depression. I asked her, "Hey, you've helped a lot of people in our church community deal with anxiety. What should I write about?" And here's what she told me to tell you: "Group, group, group, group, group." End of quote. See, she's really smart. Here's what she knows, and you might know this too: When you're stuck in your own head, when you're in the loop, when the snowball is rolling, remembering to breathe and to pray and to seek is really hard. And that's why God gave us church. Church must never, ever, ever become a place where you come and fake it, right? That's why when we pray for each other, it can never, ever, ever devolve into only, "Please keep Grandma safe as she drives to see us this weekend." This is why prayer has to be, "I'm freaking out, and I need you all. I'm not doing great; I'm depressed. Help." And that's where group is so good.

Proverbs 12:25, my last passage for this chapter, says, **"Anxiety weighs down the heart, but a kind heart cheers it up."** It's the kind word of a father who helps his daughter get out of a cycle. It's the kind word of the gospel that a friend gives to another friend saying, "Hey, just breathe with me for a bit." It's the kind word that you might share in the lobby at church saying, "Can I pray for you? Like right now—pray for you?" It's the kind word of a roommate who says, "Let's not forget Jesus is still on his throne and he is your King and he made you right with God." When we can't think of God ourselves, when our memory is clouded and our glitter is all riled up, it is sometimes the people in our lives who help us out of it. That is how we deal with almost everything, and anxiety is no exception.

If you want to know how to deal the next time worrisome thoughts come, you breathe, you pray, you seek, and you group.

There are a lot of pictures I love in my house, but I have a favorite. If you offered me a thousand dollars, I would not sell this to you. Because a few years ago, anxiety became the unwelcomed guest in my own home, and it didn't want to leave. So we bought and we framed this. Here's the image:

Courtesy of Christopher Powers (fullofeyes.com)

This is how my family deals with anxiety. We look at this picture, and we breathe. And then we pray, not just to some distant God but to our Good Shepherd. We remember we are like helpless little lambs who are defenseless against a roaring lion but we have a Good Shepherd who holds us in his hands. And we look at Jesus, who's not panicking. He's not running; he's not fighting; he's sitting at the right hand of God, where he rules over the universe and every last thing that we're worried about. He holds in his hands a pen, and he writes our stories and makes plans for our future that aren't plans to harm us but to give us hope, a future that is for sure, guaranteed, and going to be okay. But our favorite part is his hand, the hand he holds us with. That hand still bears the scar that reminds us we are forgiven for every worrisome thought. And one day soon, this same King Jesus will appear in the sky and will make all things new, even us, and even you.

Does praying in front of this picture fix it? Sometimes. Does it bring us closer to Jesus? Always. And Jesus? He's how you deal.

Points to Ponder

Gather—Evaluate this statement: The church services that are the most helpful to anxious people are those that focus on what Jesus has done for us instead of what we should do for Jesus.

Group—How might this chapter, especially the final point, encourage you as you do life with other Christians?

Grow—Study 1 Peter 5:1-11, the context of one of the Bible's most famous passages about anxiety. What do Peter's words add to the thoughts in this chapter?

Give—Studies suggest that volunteering is a wonderful way to combat anxiety and depression. The Bible adds that serving others is a wonderful way to imitate the servant heart of Jesus. How might you give a bit of your time and talents in the months to come? Pray over that question, and ask our heavenly Father for guidance.

Go—Do you know someone who is dealing with anxiety? Consider sharing this book with them or talking through the message from this chapter with them.

Prayer—God, I pray not just for my family but for every family. We all deal or know someone who deals with great anxiety. Let the truths of your Word be the water, the sun, and the fertilizer that helps the little seed of faith grow so that someday very soon those same anxious thoughts wouldn't have the same power over us. God, I love you, but you love me more. I love you now, but you loved me first. Let that love be my peace and my joy today. I pray this in the powerful name of Jesus. Amen.

Chapter 4

How to Deal With Temptation

Back in the Garden of Eden, Adam and Eve were presented with a question from the devil, and it's a question that he asks every generation: "Did God really say that?" The devil wants to tempt you to sin, so how do you deal with temptation?

How do you keep from indulging like our first parents did and ruining everything? How do you keep from plunging your life into ruin and maybe your loved ones with you, just as Adam and Eve did when they fell into sin and brought in all the pain and all the suffering and all the struggles and all the death you and I still face to this day? How do you and I deal with temptation? How will the Lord lead us from it?

Thankfully the Lord answers that *how* question in the Bible. There is so much for you and me in his Word, but we won't conquer temptation today. It will be a lifelong struggle. God will be with us, and God will give us the victory. He already has in Christ.

Even the smallest of sins is a big deal.

To me there are five different things to keep in mind when it comes to temptation. The first one is this: *Sin is serious.* That's a really important truth to embrace because you and I are sinners, aren't we? We live in a world full of brokenness, and people sin all the time. In fact, every day we fall into temptation. It's so common and so part of our lives that we might be tempted to believe it's not really that big of a deal.

But it is a big deal. Even the smallest of sins is a big deal. When you study the Bible, you see that.

Only God's Word can make that clear to us. Otherwise we would think, "As long as I don't sin big-time, then I'm okay." But it's not okay. Think about Adam and Eve. When the devil came along and tempted them, what was the object of their sin? It was a piece of fruit. Have you ever thought about that? It seems like such a small thing, so what was the big deal? They took some fruit and ate it. Yet God reveals to us in his Word that the day they ate of it, they died spiritually. And it set a course for them to die physically. Had God not intervened, they would have died eternally, and all their descendants with them. Such a small thing and yet, in God's perspective, it is everything.

You don't have to go very far in the Bible to see another case study. In Genesis chapter 4, we meet Cain, the firstborn of Adam and Eve. Based on the Hebrew, they pretty much thought he might be the Savior who was promised when they fell into sin. But Cain's little sins were bitterness and anger. They displayed themselves in a shabby offering to God, and God was disappointed. God knew where that little bit of bitterness and anger could lead, so he said this: **"Sin is crouching at your door; it desires to have you, but you must rule over it"** (verse 7). This is a passage to keep in mind when it comes to temptation. But Cain didn't care. He didn't think it was that big of a deal, and do you know where that led? Cain killed his brother Abel, and he brought a curse down upon himself. It's not that God didn't love him; God did. God would give his Son for Cain, but Cain didn't care. And in this curse, Cain began to have children. Generation after generation of unbelievers all perished, all because of a little shabby offering and some anger and bitterness. Sin is a big deal, isn't it?

Are you familiar with Eli the high priest from the Old Testament? He's the one who mentored Samuel, a great prophet, who would be the one to anoint the first and second kings of Israel. Eli was a high priest in charge of leading and modeling the faith. Do you know what his sin was? It was just a little sin, it seemed. Eli was a pushover parent. He couldn't tell his boys no. What's the big deal about such a sin? How many parents are pushovers? But because he didn't manage his kids well, Hophni and Phinehas became rebellious, even as they were priests. They gave the church a bad name by skimming the offerings and taking them for themselves. They even sexually abused the women who served alongside them. Finally, God had enough because Eli and his sons were rejecting him. I'm sure Eli was thinking, "Look, boys will be boys! They're just sowing their wild oats. What can a dad do?" Samuel had to proclaim to Eli that his whole house would perish. And that's what happened in war. Hophni and Phinehas died. The ark of the covenant, which was this important box for God's people because it represented God's presence, was lost. And upon hearing this, Eli himself died. That's a big deal!

Fast-forward just a few chapters in 1 Samuel to King Saul, the first of the kings of Israel. Do you know what his problem was? He was half-hearted when it came to the Lord. He was half-devoted to him, and Samuel called him on it: "You say you listen to the Lord, and you say you're sorry, but you don't care. You don't listen to God's commands. Saul, it's not okay to be half-hearted with the Lord God. Today he has ripped the kingdom from your hand." And God did. And Saul died. Such a little sin—being half-hearted.

Fast-forward to the New Testament to Judas. Do you know what sin he was guilty of? The sin that entangled him was a love of money. His little sin turned into betraying the Lord Jesus Christ for some silver coins.

Do you get angry? Do you ignore God? Do you love money?

How can you and I fall into such grievous sins when they usually start so small?

We need to reflect on the seriousness of our sin. What sin is threatening to entangle you in your life? What pet sins do you have? What sins do you think you can just feed a little bit because it makes you happy?

Don't follow in the footsteps of these biblical case studies. Listen to God's Word. Listen to what God said to Cain: **"Sin is crouching at your door; it desires to have you, but you must rule over it"** (Genesis 4:7). Or think about what James says: **"After desire has conceived** [after we fall into sin]**, it gives birth to sin; and sin, when it is full-grown, gives birth to death"** (1:15). Every sin leads to death. God tells us: Watch out. Take it seriously. Shake it off. Do not stay in your sin.

The second thing to keep in mind is this: *Know your weaknesses.* Know where you are struggling in temptation. Why? Because the devil is truly a studier of his prey. He's studying you right now.

This is illustrated in the Bible when the devil tries three times to tempt Jesus to sin (Luke 4:1–13). Jesus is in the wilderness 40 days and 40 nights, and he's hungry because he's been fasting out of love for the Lord God. The devil sees that, so he figures he will attack: "I can see Jesus is in great need. I will tempt him not to rely on his Father but to take these stones and turn them into bread because he can. And if I can get him to sin there over his need, I win."

Of course, Jesus, being our Savior, by the Word of God alone, defends himself and conquers. So the devil tries again. He takes Jesus to the temple grounds, and if you know your Old Testament history, you know the temple was the symbol of God's presence; his protective care. He takes Jesus to the very highest part of the temple and proclaims to him the very Word of God that Jesus so loves. He says, "You know, if you love the Word of God so much and if you're truly God's Son, let's see if he's here to protect you or not, because if you're to save the world, truly, you need to know he's present. So throw yourself down because Psalm 91 says, 'He will command his angels concerning you to guard you in all your ways so that your foot does not strike up against a stone.'" But Jesus, using the Word of God, prevails. He conquers. Even in the face of his fear.

But the devil tries again. He's been studying his prey. The devil somehow takes Jesus to this high mountain, and I don't know how he did it, but he showed him all the kingdoms of the world. Think about how tempting this was! That's what Jesus came for. Jesus came to rule over all things, to be our gracious King, to save us in mercy and grace, and to give us life. He came to be King. And who was sitting on the throne of this world? The devil. The devil simply offers this: "Jesus, I know you're suffering, and I know the road to victory for you means immense suffering."

Jesus knows a cross is at the end of that road, so the devil says, "Let's cut to the quick. You want to reign? Here, I'll hand over the reins; I'll give you back your throne. Just do this one thing for me. Just worship me like you do your Father. I'll give it all to you, and no one gets hurt. What do you say?" Jesus, by the Word of God, defends himself and gives us the victory.

The devil is aiming for your needs and your fears and your wants.

Do you see how clever the devil is? Do you see how he was studying Jesus as he studies you and me? Here are the areas then that we learn the devil aims for in your life and in mine. The devil is aiming for your needs and your fears and your wants. Do you know what you need? What are your greatest fears in this life? What are your greatest wants? You can be sure the devil will come to you on all those things, and he will not give up until you defend yourself with the Word. We need to study the Bible. This was the Lord's only defense; this must be our defense too.

Here's the third thing to remember when it comes to temptation: *Don't rest on your laurels.* Don't rest on the accomplishments you could be proud of in this life, or you might begin to think that God owes you life and salvation and heaven because you're such a good person or you've done this or that. Your pride is your laurels. In 1 Corinthians 10:12, the apostle Paul says it this way: **"If you think you are standing firm, be careful that you don't fall."**

Paul also presents a case study from the Old Testament. Moses was the great deliverer of Israel out of Egypt. They were in slavery for four hundred years, and God sent Moses. Through ten miraculous plagues, the Israelites were delivered out of that land of slavery. Through the miraculous parting of the Red Sea—you can read about this in Exodus chapters 1 through 20—they received freedom. And God was bringing them along in the wilderness to the Promise Land. The Israelites had it all.

Now you'd think if there was any generation that could withstand temptation, it would be that generation. But only two of them made it to the Promise Land (Joshua and Caleb; see Numbers 14:30). That's it. The rest perished in the wilderness under God's judgment. How is that? Because of pride. They were so puffed up, thinking that God miraculously worked out all these things because of who they were, the children of Abraham, good people. They got so arrogant that they grumbled against the Lord God and anything that Moses said. They got so arrogant that they wanted to go back to Egypt because they thought it was better to be back in slavery in Egypt than to have to listen to God and his Word and Moses.

Could you and I fall the same way? Is it possible that you and I, who know Jesus, could think so much of ourselves that somehow we would think he owes us the salvation he provides? Maybe if you come from a family who for generations has been Christian, you could get so prideful and arrogant that you think it doesn't really matter how you live your life or what you do; God owes you. You're his child; you know Jesus, your ticket to heaven. You can live as you want.

What Paul said in 1 Corinthians, Solomon said in Proverbs: **"Pride brings a person low, but the lowly in spirit gain honor"** (29:23). I want to encourage you, as you battle with temptation, don't rest on your laurels. Don't think you're strong enough to handle it. Don't think God somehow owes you, so you can live as you want. Don't be prideful. Humbly call out to the Lord God: "Lead me far from temptation. Deliver me from evil."

Which leads to the fourth thing we want to embrace when it comes to temptation. *I want you to remember the sacrificial cost of Jesus.* This is how we deal with temptation. Connect the dots between Christ's love, his sacrifice, and your daily struggle with temptation.

Whenever you're battling temptation and you're about to sin, think of Jesus, bloodied and beaten and dying on a cross. Think of him saying, "Father, forgive them. They don't know what they're doing." Think about how he was separated from God so you never would be and so you would find the strength to keep fighting against that temptation, to be free from that sin. You see, you look at your Savior Jesus and you look at that sin and you see your great reward, and that sin has nothing but empty promises to offer. And there's your strength and mind. Yes, think of your Savior

Jesus on the cross. And there you overcome, whether or not you fall.

So remember that sacrificial cost to Jesus, and it will inspire in your heart a desire, just like Joseph in the Old Testament. When Joseph was tempted to sleep with Potiphar's wife, he thought of the love of God, that sacrificial cost, which was promised to him and he cried out, **"How then could I do such a wicked thing and sin against God?"** (Genesis 39:9). And he ran. You see, that's the love of God and the power of the gospel when we think of Christ on the cross. That is the power to overcome; that's how we deal.

The apostle Paul said it this way in Titus 2:11,12: **"For the grace of God has appeared that offers salvation."** That grace is the love of Christ on the cross. It's finally come, and all who believe in it are saved. Not only does it land us in heaven, but Paul says it teaches us **"to say 'No' to ungodliness and worldly passions, and to live self-controlled, upright and godly lives in this present age."** Praise God, that's the power of the gospel.

Which leads me to my last thought for this chapter. *The final thing to help deal with temptation is to take up the full armor of God.* And we definitely don't want to soldier alone. Paul talks about this in Ephesians 6:10-18.

Your identity is in Christ.

First, he reminds us that we're in a war. Our battle is not against flesh and blood but against the devil and his demons. But in this armor of God, you have nothing to fear.

So what's the first piece of armor? It's the helmet of salvation. It means keep your focus on Christ above. Do not get so earthly minded that you lose it all; your reward is yet to come. Your identity is in Christ, so keep your head up and keep your head in the game and fight the battle God has called you to, knowing that Christ is your victory.

Then put on the breastplate of righteousness. Righteousness is something God gifts us in Christ. All the good we ought to do but don't do and the forgiveness of sins are all packed in this protection over our hearts. This is where God drives out our old hearts, our old sinful self, and gives us his own beating heart, where he alone knows what is right, where he alone defines good and evil. Keep that over your heart. Have a heart after God's. Don't just follow your feelings but live according to that right path and follow Christ.

Then pick up the shield of faith. Faith is in all the promises of God he has for you, especially in the darker days when it looks like God maybe isn't even there. And how do you keep your faith strong? By getting into God's Word and clinging to his promises. That shield of faith is how you can extinguish all the flaming arrows of doubt and accusation the devil throws at you.

Keep it all together by the belt of truth. God's Word is truth. God's Word is what holds us together. Christ is the Way and the Truth and the Life. Listen to him. Go to the Scriptures. Seek him out, and he will define all things as true or false. Live in that truth, and keep your feet fitted with the readiness of the gospel of peace. Let the good news of Christ in regard to how you live for God and how you interact with others be what moves you and motivates you. Don't let anything else do that; not power, not money, not sex, not whatever influence, not anything of this world but only the gospel.

Next take up the sword of the Spirit, which is the Word of God. I love that because it's not just a defensive position; a sword causes you to go on the offensive. You are not a victim; you're a victor. And the gates of hell will not stand up against the Word of God, which is what you have in your hand. You can demolish all strongholds, all arguments that oppose Christ, and you can cause all your thoughts to be submitted to Christ who gives you the victory.

Finally, pray. Pray for not only your deliverance from temptation but for others too. And this is the point about not soldiering alone. If you're in war, don't do it alone; you can't. In fact, some would suggest that if you try to do this on your own, you will perish. But if you do it with one another, do life together, you will be stronger.

I've given you a lot to think about, but I don't want you to be overwhelmed. Here's one last passage for encouragement: **"No temptation has overtaken you except what is common to mankind."** You're not alone; you're not strange for feeling overwhelmed. But even better, **"God is faithful; he will not let you be tempted beyond what you can bear. But when you are tempted, he will also provide a way out so that you can endure"** (1 Corinthians 10:13).

God makes this beautiful promise to you, and he will keep it. You don't need to be afraid. Keep Christ as your focus. He will give you the strength to conquer in the battle what he already has conquered by his empty grave. That's how you deal with temptation.

Points to Ponder

Gather—How would you explain to a family member or friend how worshiping Jesus with other Christians helps you with temptation?

Group—Do you agree that growing closer to other Christians and being vulnerable about your struggles with temptation is essential to dealing with temptation? Why or why not?

Grow—Have you ever thought about putting a visual reminder (sticky note, etc.) somewhere in your home to remind you about fighting temptation? Where might you put that reminder?

Go—Do you know someone drowning in temptation and sin? How might you share this chapter with them?

Prayer—Heavenly Father, I come before you today and thank you. You have given me so much to think about in your Word, and I ask then that you would continue to cause these truths to penetrate my heart so I might always do battle and, in Christ, find the victory. Amen.

Chapter 5
How to Deal With Shame

A while back I tried to assemble the best Bible study ever. I had this really brilliant plan. I'd been meeting people in different areas of my life, and I noticed all these people had something really big and really difficult in their lives. There was drug addiction, alcoholism, pornography, sexual sin, adultery, and problems in marriage. I thought to myself, "What would happen if I could get all these people in the same room and we could open a Bible and we could talk about God and we could talk about life?" I know all these people well enough. None of us is a saint, and we've all got baggage, so there's no one to impress. We'd just be real before each other, before God. That was my plan, but it didn't work.

I invited the people, and they came to the study. We opened the Bible and talked about Jesus. We prayed for each other and talked about the ups and downs, but do you know what never came up? That stuff. It wasn't my place to betray anyone's confidence or reveal a secret that someone had told the pastor, but week after week, I just kept thinking to myself, "Come on. Come on. Just say it. Because once you say it, she's going to say it. And once you say it, he's going to say, 'Me too.' Then this is going to be the best Bible study ever."

But they didn't say it. And I get it. Have you ever been with a really good friend or with some good people from church and they ask you how you are doing and how life is going? You talk about life and some ups and some downs, but the one thing you really need to talk about, you don't? That feeling, when you're around pretty good people—not dangerous people or gossipy people—but pretty good people, and you're scared to say that one thing—that's what I call shame. Shame is the thing that says, "*Shh*, let's not bring that up. Let's not talk about that, not right now, not with these people, not right here." Shame is something you and I need to learn how to deal with.

Now I'm not sure of your spiritual story, but I've been on both sides of shame. I've kept secrets, and I've revealed them. I've struggled with sins by myself, and I've openly confessed them. And as difficult as it is to cross over that line into honesty, it is one of the most liberating, helpful, beautiful things that you can experience in the church. But here's the thing: Shame is really hard in the church. I'm not sure what it all is, but I have a hunch it's this: In the church, we have incredibly high moral standards. We love the teachings of Jesus; we love what he said about self-control and generosity, about love and about purity. We love the biblical teachings on love and respect and unity and healthy families, and I think because we push that up so high, when people like you and me fall short of that standard, we instinctively feel shame. As if we're not living up to it;

> **We keep our secrets, and we wonder deep down if we belong.**

we're not being the good church people, the holy Christian people, and so we kind of keep it quiet and pray about it and battle it by ourselves. We keep our secrets, and we wonder deep down if we belong.

So I have one big goal. I want to persuade you to cross the line. I want to show you the beautiful result of what happens when a Christian community, or just a Christian family, can learn how to deal with shame. It will not be easy. It might be the scariest thing you've ever done. I hope I can persuade you to deal with shame along with a community of people, because communities of people are the only way to deal with shame.

While a lot of things can make you and me feel embarrassed or humiliated or ashamed, I think there are four particular things in my experience that people don't want to talk about. The first very powerful type of shame is legal shame. When your sins and transgressions have crossed a legal line, it can be really tough to talk about. For example, if in your past you spent time behind bars, it's hard to apply for an apartment or go on a first date because someone could look up your legal history on the internet. You hope deep down they don't find out about that part of your past. You might worry about what you're going to wear to church because you've got an ankle bracelet. If your parole officer texts you, you might be embarrassed to tell your friends who it is.

There can be a deep sense of shame if you've crossed a legal line, especially if the crime you've committed has hurt other people. You may have embarrassed your family. If your time in jail made you miss your son's birthday or a really big moment, it is very easy to feel shame. How many church services have you been to where someone talks about being in prison or jail or about a loved one who is? Probably not many or none. That's stuff we don't generally talk about. But we need to.

Another kind of shame we need to talk about is chemical shame. If your struggle spiritually has been with a chemical substance—with alcohol, pills, narcotics, drugs—that is something we need to talk about. I've got to tell you, in our community and in our church community, this is everywhere, but it's tough to bring up. If you can't have a glass of wine with the ladies from church like the other normies do because you know one's going to turn into seven, that's tough to admit. If friends are going out afterward for pizza and beer and you just know you can't walk into a bar because you know where that's going to lead, that's tough to confess. If you go to Bible study and all that week you've been struggling with taking pills that you really don't need and shouldn't have been prescribed, that's tough to talk about.

When you've been high and it wasn't just back in college with a little weed, but it was last weekend and something more than weed. If you've tried coke, if you've hit up heroin, and if you've done meth, that's tough to talk about in church. If you told someone about it, they might wonder if you've been down that road before and what would happen if you got hooked again? They might take a step away, and you'd feel shame.

If all that wasn't enough, there's relational shame. If your family history, past or present, is messy, you might feel relational shame. I actually notice this all the time when divorce happens in our church. A couple is a huge part of our spiritual community, things get off track, they separate, they divorce, and the time they most need to be in church for encouragement and support and the time when they're most broken and wounded is the time they don't even want to come, right? What if you've been through a divorce or two or your mom and dad weren't the perfect couple or you grew up with a step-this and a step-that or there was dad's girlfriend and mom's other boyfriend? When you come to church where it's about husband and wife and love and respect and beautiful kids baptized and confirmed, it's tough. When you don't come from a great family, you feel shame. You might see church families who come in their coordinated church outfits. They do the family trips to Florida with the matching neon T-shirts, and you just know that's not how you grew up; that's not your family. You barely talked to each other, and you kind of feel like you don't belong.

Then there's the worst shame of all. It's a shame I'm

not sure existed in the first century with the Greeks and the Romans, but in the 21st century with Americans, it absolutely does. There's legal shame, there's chemical shame, there's relational shame, and can you guess the last kind of shame? There's sexual shame.

The Bible frequently talks about orgies, lust, prostitution, and the like, but when's the last time you had coffee with the ladies from church and talked about that? If lust is your struggle, if you're hooked on porn, if you compulsively masturbate, when's the last time someone prayed for you for that? If you've lost track of the number of sexual partners you've had or you can count exactly how many sexual partners you've had, when's the last time someone helped you with that? If you know what it's like to pay a prostitute, to call a hotline, to walk in a parking lot after having been in a strip club, how do you talk about that?

Here's what you should know. The stuff I just talked about has happened in churches. You don't have to be a megachurch with 10,000 attendees; this stuff happens all the time in churches, but you might not have known it. The reason is shame.

I want to help you deal with shame. As Christians, we do not want to be secret keepers. We want to be the kind of people who step out of the darkness and into the light and experience the shame-erasing power of Jesus. We don't want to hide and pray behind closed doors so no one else knows; we want to step out into real community. We want to do life with one another so we don't have to do this alone anymore. We can pray and encourage, forgive and support in Jesus' name.

So I want to help you deal with shame. And to do so, I looked up every single passage in the Bible that uses the words *shame, shamed,* or *ashamed.* Do you know what I found out? Shame is a really complex issue to write about. So instead of giving you the whole biblical teaching on shame, I want to make just one main point. This is it:

Your heavenly Father, who adores you as his kid, says this: Be ashamed temporarily.

The world would say that the way we should deal with shame is we should all just be okay. You're okay. I'm okay. We're all good. Nobody's perfect, so there's no shame. Everyone's welcome here; you belong. But the Bible wouldn't say that. The Bible instead says this: Be ashamed temporarily.

The Bible instead says this: Be ashamed temporarily.

Let me prove it to you. In the Old Testament, the prophet Jeremiah preached to a bunch of people who looked pretty religious. They went to church, they said their prayers, and they offered their sacrifices. They did not love the poor, and their courts were not places of justice and fairness. People who had more money got away with murder, and people went to church the next Sunday because they belonged with God, right? And Jeremiah said these words: **"Are they ashamed of their detestable conduct? No, they have no shame at all; they do not even know how to blush"** (6:15). Jeremiah said that blushing is sometimes a blessing. When you can do something detestable, something shameful, and just smile up at God, that's not a sign of spiritual health but a major red flag. If you're into church lingo, this is what we call living in sin or a life that lacks repentance. When we do something that God detests and don't feel shame, humiliation, or embarrassment about it, Jeremiah says we have no shame at all. That's not a good thing.

That's why if you jump ahead to the New Testament, the apostle Paul actually used the power of shame to correct a wayward church. In the New Testament, the apostle Paul started a church in the Greek city of Corinth. And after he left, another pastor came to shepherd the church. Paul heard a rumor that two members of the church were dragging each other to court. They couldn't work it out, so they lawyered up and went to court. When Paul heard about it, do you know what he said? "You should be ashamed. You're supposed to be the people who will sacrifice everything because you have God. You're dragging this drama out in front of a world that doesn't even believe in Jesus." Paul said this in 1 Corinthians 6: **"I say this to shame you. Is it possible that there is nobody among you wise enough to judge a dispute between believers?"** (verse 5). Paul said shame, that feeling of humiliation, has a rightful place when people aren't repenting of sins.

I know it's a heavy message to share with you, but doesn't it make sense? If I wanted to have any kind of friendship or relationship with you and I was doing something that hurt you and felt no grief or sorrow about it, could we actually be close? It makes me think of a guy I met years ago. Let's call him "the strip club fiancé." There was this young woman from my church who got engaged. The guy she was in love with was not a Christian, and he was not ashamed of any of it. They came into my office to talk, and I was trying to get to know him and trying to make some small talk and I said to him, "So what do you like to do?"

He smirked back and said, "Strip clubs." And before he and I had a few words, I glanced over at his fiancée and felt so bad for her.

Do people who are engaged struggle with sexual sin? For sure. Do some even struggle so much they end up in a strip club? For sure. But the fact that he didn't struggle with it or did it without blushing or embarrassment, how in the world would that work?

Afterward, through my office window, I could see them by their car. I couldn't hear their conversation, but I remember she was standing there and he was doing all the talking. I thought to myself, "Without shame, it is impossible for a relationship to survive."

That's what I want you to get from this chapter: Be ashamed. If you choose something before God, be ashamed. If when you're stressed you turn to a drug, to a bottle, to a click, to a purchase, to work, to numbing yourself with whatever, if that's your functional savior, be ashamed. The Bible sometimes wants us to grieve and to wail and to mourn. If God is infinitely good and pure, every time we don't choose to love him is infinitely offensive. Don't run to some happy, clappy church that will never convict you of your sin. It might feel good in the moment, but it does not feel good to God. "Have they no shame?" God says. "They don't know how to blush." So learn to blush. Take seriously the goodness, the holiness, and the commands of God and be ashamed.

Temporarily.

If Christianity was about long-term shame, I'd bounce. If I came to church and some pastor made me feel bad in the beginning, in the middle, and at the end, I wouldn't come back. But the best news I have for you is that God allows us to feel shame, but not for long. He allows us to cry tears of repentance, but soon **God allows us to feel shame, but not for long.** he wipes them away. Because from the first sinner right up to you and me, God has been in the business of making sure that the feeling of shame is not forever.

I got to experience that in one of the more important days of my life. You may know that a part of my story is an addiction. In my past I gave into a sexual sin, pornography, and did not turn away from it. I hid it and covered it up, until one day I told a really good friend. I was so reluctant, but finally—poof—I said it. And he did not put me to shame. In one of the most important moments of my spiritual story, there was a guy who acted a lot like God and made sure that my remorse did not remain. He took my shame to the only place where shame can really be dealt with, the cross where Jesus bled.

You see, this is what the Christian faith is all about. We come to God in remorse, feeling like we don't belong, and he does the craziest thing and assures us that we do. Hasn't he been doing that since the start?

Do you know the story of Adam and Eve in the Bible? Adam and Eve sinned against God. They were so ashamed that they ran and hid; they were naked and exposed. But do you know what God did? He found them, covered their shame, and gave them a promise about Jesus. He said to the devil, "No, no, no, no. You did it. But not for long. You made my kids run and hide but not forever. You separated them from me, but I'm not going to let that happen." In that moment, God gave the first shamed people the antidote for shame. He promised a Savior to come, one born of a woman, who would crush the shame giver's head, which is exactly what he did.

I love this passage from the book of Hebrews. Speaking of Jesus, it says, **"For the joy set before him he endured the cross, scorning its shame, and sat down at the right hand of the throne of God"** (12:2). The reason Jesus died on a cross instead of peacefully in his sleep was so that you and I wouldn't have to live with shame. All the humiliation, the embarrassment, the feeling of not belonging—he wanted to drag it to an old rugged cross and scorn it, mock it, nail it, and leave it behind. Jesus so badly wanted joy for you that he was willing to do that. And before his last breath, he said,

"It's finished. It's dealt with. It's done." And he rose from the grave to prove that it's true.

That's why I have the sincere privilege of writing this: God's not ashamed. He knows the story. He knows the struggle. He knows your legal record. He doesn't have to check the internet to find out. He knows what happened. He knows when you got high and how many times. He knows all of it. But do you know what God does not feel about you? Shame.

Let me prove it with three Bible passages. Here's the first one: **"Therefore God is not ashamed to be called their God"** (Hebrews 11:16). Have you noticed these days when some celebrity really messes up morally, when he tweets something really stupid or they find something in her high school yearbook, everyone takes a step back, every sponsor cuts ties, every director chops them from the movie. God's not like that. He doesn't cancel us; he doesn't take a step back.

I love this: God himself, the holy perfect God, is not ashamed or embarrassed to be called our God. When you say, "That's my God; that's my Savior," he does not say, "Eh, no."

He says, "Yes, I am. And you're my child." In my Father's house, there is a place for me. With your history, past, story, there's a place for you too. And when you see the Father's face, Jesus shows up. When the holy angels gather around, Jesus doesn't take a step back from you. No, look at Hebrews 2:11. It says, **"So Jesus is not ashamed to call them brothers and sisters."** He's not embarrassed to belong to us.

The book of Romans leaves us with this incredible promise: **"Anyone who believes in Jesus will never be put to shame"** (10:11). Never. Through Jesus, we're cleansed, we're made holy, we run out of the grave of secrecy, and we admit, "Here's what I did. Here's who I've been." But God is not ashamed. "Yeah, I hate that I did that, but I love it because Jesus did this. I'm not going to hide. I'm not going to fake it.

I'm done with image management. I'm done with trying to impress you or prove I'm better than you might think I am. Here's the sinner I am, and here's the saint Jesus made me to be." So week after week and day after day, we lift up the cross of Jesus. We cling and praise the blood of Jesus because in him we will never, ever, ever be put to shame.

So maybe next time the Bible study will work. Maybe I'll invite you, and you'll remember this. And you'll say, "So I need help with . . ." and he'll say, "Me too." And he'll say, "I've been there." And she'll say, "I'll pray." And we'll become the kind of people who feel shame but not for long. God, make it so.

Points to Ponder

Gather—Evaluate the following statement: For a church to deal properly with shame, the pastors need to regularly talk about *everything.*

Group—Agree/Disagree: It is impossible to carry out God's beautiful commands to "pray for one another," "encourage one another," and "bear one another's burdens" if shame is causing us to keep secrets. If you agree, what can you personally do to deal with shame in your circle of friends?

Grow—The Bible says, **"Anyone who believes in** [Jesus] **will never be put to shame"** (Romans 10:11). What is your favorite word in this passage? Why?

Give—Do you have an intentional plan to give a set percentage of your income to the poor and to the spread of the gospel? If not, don't be ashamed to ask another Christian how joyful giving works.

Go—Can you think of someone who believes they are too broken to belong with other Christians? Talk to them and share the content of this chapter with them.

Prayer—Dear God, rid me of pride, of a holier-than-thou spirit. Instead, clothe me with compassion just like you clothe me with the righteousness of your Son. Thank you, God, for those who taught me about grace. Thank you for the inheritance of mercy that I have and a no-strings-attached love in the gospel. I love you, God, and I want to love others well. Help me learn how to deal with shame. Amen.

Chapter 6
How to Deal With Apathy

I'm very aware of the challenges and struggles people have had or are having in this world. I don't know your individual struggles, but I know you have them. So I don't want to minimize any of that with my next statement.

But in the midst of all those struggles, sometimes we forget to talk about the silver linings. I'm talking about the blessings you've found and experienced and seen maybe in your life, even in the midst of something so difficult and challenging and devastating. I think that's an important thing for us to look at. I think it's important, especially as we dive into this chapter, because when we can see the little blessings, the silver linings, we see what we can learn, even in difficulties.

For example, I think near the top of the list of one of the things every one of us can say we've learned is perspective. Here's an example—During the time we were locked down in our country because of COVID, I heard things like this: "Pastor, I know this is bad. I know this is hard. People are dealing with the difficulties, and it's a challenge to be under the same roof working from home with kids doing school at home, but we've learned something, Pastor. We've learned there's something called quantity time that is just as important as quality time. Our family actually ate every meal together at night for a stretch of 12 weeks like never before." I've heard some husbands and wives talk about their relationships growing, even though there were challenges.

I'm bringing up the silver lining/blessing of perspective because it revealed something to me: When there are distractions in our lives, we let little things creep in that get in the way of big things. For example, I don't think any child or grandchild wants to give their loved ones the impression they aren't important or they don't matter. But life gets busy, and the priority of visiting parents or grandparents becomes something we care less and less about or forget. I don't think any spouse would say it's not important to spend quantity time with family, but work comes in and obligations come in. We get pulled this way and that way and forget the importance of it and don't care about it as much.

Apathy is tricky because it creeps in.

I think that's really the underlying issue of this chapter's topic, dealing with apathy. The issue of apathy is one that is ever present. Apathy is tricky because it creeps in. It's not easy to see. It doesn't hit us like a ton of bricks; it creeps in slowly and over time affects our lives. It affects our souls.

Before we go further, I want to define *apathy* clearly. *Apathy* comes from the Greek word *pathos*. *Pathos* means "emotion or passion." Anything in the Greek language with an *"a"* in front of it is a negative, lacking emotion, lacking passion. So when we say the word *apathy*, what we're really talking about is someone who lacks emotion, lacks passion, lacks a concern for something or someone. Sometimes people refer to it as a feeling of indifference. Apathy comes from someone who says, "I don't care." In fact, they add one more phrase to it: "I don't care that I don't care." That is apathy.

I want you to dig in and really wrestle with this question: Where are the areas of your life right now that that's true? Maybe it's work. Maybe it's politics. Maybe it's your marriage. Where do you hear yourself saying or thinking, "I just don't care"?

Here's the danger in apathy and why you need to address it: Apathy is something that creeps in slowly and takes us down a path of not caring as much as we should, losing our emotion or passion for something that we should. It leads us to a place where we don't care that we don't care anymore. Apathy is destructive for this life.

One of the reasons why apathy creeps into people's lives is familiarity. You and I lose the awe and feeling for something that we once had; we lose the passion. This happens in marriage. Unlike people who are dating, some couples lose the passion after ten years of being married. People come into my office and want to talk to me. These aren't situations where someone has crossed the line, violated what God says marriage is to be. They come in and say, "Pastor, I just don't love that person anymore. I don't care. I'm at a point where I don't care that I don't care, so I'm going to get a divorce."

That's apathy; it can destroy relationships.

They don't have passion for their spouse anymore and want to walk down a different path. That's apathy; it can destroy relationships. Familiarity can do that.

You know what else can do it? Being desensitized to something. Thirty years ago my parents never let me watch *Three's Company*. Maybe you remember that one? People lived together, and there were sexual innuendos. My parents were like, "Bad! Horrible! Bad!" But now my parents would applaud that compared to what's on TV. My daughter and son-in-law won't watch certain Netflix shows, and I might say, "I watch that. That doesn't bother me." We've become desensitized to things; we don't care that we don't care anymore about the things we see.

Or think about work. Have you accepted mediocrity? You don't care that you don't care. Your boss changed your work situation or told you that you need to take a furlough. Maybe you need to take a pay cut. Maybe you didn't get a raise this year, but you saw the company report. They made a million dollars more than they made the year before, and now you're willing to accept mediocrity at work, to surf more than actually do the job. You just don't care that you don't care.

I could go on with the list, but I think it's clear that apathy is a destructive thing in this life for us socially, relationally, and for our work. I also hope you'll see that none of those areas of life are separated for us as Christians from our relationship with God. All those things are part of our godly callings to use our gifts and talents to God's glory, to work and do our best wherever we are employed, to give our best and love in relationships like God has called us to love. It's a destructive thing for this life when apathy creeps in. Even more important, it can be deadly for the soul.

Do you know what happens when you start not caring about not caring? In all those different areas and in most of those ways, you forget about your identity. You forget about your purpose, you forget about your mission, and you forget all those godly callings God has given to you in your life as a Christian. When you start walking down that path, it endangers you physically, spiritually, and emotionally.

If you haven't read enough, let God speak to you. Apathy is something Christian churches have identified for thousands of years. Have you ever heard of the Seven Deadly Sins (pride, greed, lust, envy, gluttony, wrath, and sloth)? There's one called sloth. Some people call it laziness, but sloth is basically apathy. The Christian church said the definition of sloth is someone who lacks love and doesn't do the things that God would say they should. They don't do good. And that's literally what God is talking about when he talks about apathy. We don't do the good things that God wants us to do that bless others and are part of our relationship with him.

Do you know what God thinks about that? He says this: **"If anyone . . . knows the good they ought to do and doesn't do it, it is sin for them"** (James 4:17). Can you see how all the topics in this book are woven together? A previous chapter talked about how to deal with temptation. At the beginning, temptation is a big deal because when we don't fight temptation, when we don't deal with temptation, when we don't address temptation, it leads us to sin. And when we sin, it gives birth to death. It's spiritually deadly. And right in the Bible, God says, **"If anyone . . . knows the good they ought to do and doesn't do it, it is sin for them."** Apathy isn't ignorance, someone who doesn't know what they're doing. It's not complacency, where you're satisfied with the status quo. No. Apathy is literally knowing the good that God would have you do and saying, "I don't care. I'm not going to do it." Can you see the danger in your spiritual life and your relationship with God? God calls us to do good things. He calls us to help our neighbors, to help those who are in need, but have you ever found yourself saying, "That's not my job. I don't care. Let someone else do it"?

Or think what God says about guarding people's reputations. There are some in your life who are just slaughtering another person's good name. You see it online; you hear it in their words. Over and over again it comes up, and God says the good thing to do is to defend the person who is being talked about in a mean way. But you simply say, "Not my job. I've had enough of it. I don't care."

What is the good thing God has called you to do? What are the good things God has laid out in his Word that right now you're not doing because you don't care? God calls it sin, and you and I need to recognize it, see it, and deal with it. If we don't deal with those good things that God has called us to do (the life he's called us to live, the way in which he longs for us to use our talents and our gifts and our time, the good things he's called us to speak into or speak up for), then the mission of God is undermined because we don't take the opportunity for others to see the love of Jesus in our lives.

The more we don't care that we don't care can lead us to not caring about the One we should care about the most. For an example of apathy in the Bible, read the story and the history of God's people in the Old Testament. Here's an example from the prophet Hosea: **"When I [God] fed them, they were satisfied; when they were satisfied, they became proud; then they forgot me"** (13:6). God did good things to provide for the Israelites in the wilderness. He brought them out of Egypt and provided for them a land flowing with milk and honey; he helped them conquer that land and blessed them with it. When he fed them, they were satisfied, and when they were satisfied, they became proud. In came the sin of pride. They cared more about themselves than God. They were more passionate about themselves than they were about God. They forgot him. They didn't care that they didn't care about God.

The Bible is full of passages that tell us what it means not to care about God: an eternity away from him. I pray you can see in your life where there are places where you haven't done the good that God's called you to do. Helping others who are in need, speaking up for the truth, addressing sin when it is real, doing in love all the good that God has called you to do. Maybe right now you're not caring about the way you should be, or maybe you're on the verge of not caring that you don't care. Maybe it's sin in your life that you're apathetic to that you're rationalizing or minimizing. Here's the truth that God said in Revelation 3:15: **"I know your**

deeds." It may have crept in; you may not be aware of it. But God sees it and knows it. He says, I know **"that you are neither cold nor hot** [you're not passionate and emotional for the things I care about; you're not on fire for me. You're not completely cold, and you're not dead in your faith 100%]. **I wish you were either one or the other!"** In other words, "I hate lukewarm," God says. "I hate apathy. There's no worse place to be than someone who doesn't care that they don't care." And **"because you're lukewarm—neither hot nor cold—I am about to spit you out of my mouth"** (verse 16).

That hits to the heart; that's how God feels about it. And I wonder if we need to get perspective on something that is so vitally important to dealing with the sin of apathy: our roots of faith. Has your daily time with God increased, stayed the same, or gotten worse lately? Have you seen your devotional time with God decrease because of your online presence? Or what about going to church? Have you gotten complacent? Have you maybe taken advantage of the option and opportunity to stay at home and to worship from home and gotten okay with that? As great as it is, it doesn't replace what we do in person. And that's not to say that it's always wrong to worship at home. But have you allowed worship to slip, maybe to be less passionate about it, to care less about that hour that you're giving?

Or how about telling others about Jesus? Do you make excuses about how hard it is? Or have you set it to the side for a while until you feel better about it?

Do you know who loves apathy? When you're not passionate about the things God is passionate about, when you're not emotionally invested and passionate for the faith roots that are so vital and important, do you know who likes lukewarm? The devil loves it because the slow creep only keeps going and going and going until you get to the bad place where you don't care. The devil loves that.

I'm concerned that apathy has crept into our lives. But that's why I'm thankful that if right now your heart is convicted, if apathy has crept in somewhere, then you and I can shed the light on it and see what God says about how to deal with it.

I'm concerned that apathy has crept into our lives.

So what would God have us do to go from people who have apathy to people who are filled with passion and emotions for what he is passionate about? How do we do that?

First, I want to give you the antidote for apathy. It's how to go from being someone desensitized to someone who's aware and gains perspective. How do we not allow boredom to creep in? How do we not allow isolation to happen? Here's how to do it:

"Therefore, since we are surrounded by such a great cloud of witnesses, let us throw off everything that hinders and the sin that so easily entangles" (Hebrews 12:1). The writer to the Hebrews says to "throw off" what hinders us. One of those sins that so easily entangles is apathy. Throw it all off, and **"let us run with perseverance the race marked out for us."** The journey we're on in life is the time we have on earth to carry out all the things God has called us to do. Here's how we fix apathy, according to Hebrews 12:2: We fix our eyes on Jesus. He went to a cross, lived a perfect life, rose from the dead, and is ascended into heaven where he rules over all things for our good. He's the One who calls us to do good and is ruling over all things for your good and mine.

Then the author of the Hebrews says this also in verse 2: **"For the joy set before him he endured the cross, scorning its shame, and sat down at the right hand of the throne of God."** Our Savior was passionate about God's mission to rescue you and me. He was filled with the emotion of joy because he knew what it would mean for us. He knew that what he was going to do would make you and me good, perfect, and holy in the eyes of God. There was never a moment when he got bored with the mission. There was never a moment when he allowed familiarity to cloud his judgment. There was never a time when he got desensitized by what he saw. No, Jesus cared.

Look at how he lived; look at how he loved. The things that God called good, the things that God was passionate about—loving those who were hurting—Jesus did those things. Think of the times when he had compassion for those who were like sheep without a shepherd. Jesus was not apathetic ever. He stopped and paused when his schedule was full. He cared. The people who were in need and the people who were different, the people who were outcasts, do you know what Jesus did? He went to their homes. He loved them. That's Jesus. He didn't just stand by and say, "I don't care." Instead, he went to a cross where he was nailed and died because he was passionate about you because he cares.

The antidote to apathy is awe.

"Consider him who endured such opposition from sinners, so that you will not grow weary and lose heart" (Hebrews 12:3). That's really what apathy boils down to. You get weary, you get worn out, you get bored, you get complacent, and you get desensitized.

The world beats us down. We get weary, we get burdened, and we get distracted. Apathy creeps in. What's the remedy; what's the antidote? Jesus. Here's how I want you to remember it. The antidote to apathy is awe. Don't lose your awe for the things that are amazing because you get familiar with them.

It's like if you signed up for an Airbnb. You found a place near water. You've got an amazing porch on the back, and you're going to get there and sit on that porch and watch the sunset go down. You'll be in awe of it because it's not familiar; it's beautiful. But do you know what the people who put their house on Airbnb think about that? Meh. They're not in awe of it; they see it every day. They built a beautiful home, they lived in it for a while, and it's become normal. It's familiar; they lost the awe of it.

When God calls us to do good, sadly, sometimes we lose the awe of God, the amazing picture of the cross of our Savior Jesus, where he went for you and for me to pay for all our sins. We're not as passionate about that. I've been a Christian 48 years of my life. My parents took me to a font ten days in. And do you know what I sometimes do? I go through the motions; I do. I take it for granted. I study the Word every day, but my studying isn't as great as it could be. Apathy so easily can creep in when we take for granted the things that are so familiar.

We can never let the amazing love of God, the grace of God, the cross of Jesus Christ be something we ever lose our awe for. Stop and pause every morning to celebrate the amazing love of God. Thank God every day for another day of grace. Somewhere in the middle of your day, think about what it means for you that one day you're going to be in heaven!

Many of us don't get that perspective until we get close to death. I visited with a member of our church recently and he asked, "Pastor, is there any way you can help me get there sooner?" He just wanted to be in heaven sooner. People like him love their families and will miss them, but they're at a point where they're so excited to see God.

I need some more of that in my life every day, don't you? Do you know how you get that, how to find that antidote?

How do you get awe that increases; how do you stop the slow creep that takes you down the road to being apathetic toward the things God wants you to do? You do the slow work every day of being rooted in God's Word. Start with one thing—spend a few minutes in God's Word or read a daily devotion. It doesn't have to be a lot. Spend one more minute each day this week. And then the next week, do the same. If you don't **have a devotional life right now, can you start with just five minutes with God?** Every day you can increase the awe that you have for God, the amazing love that God has for you!

If you're not connected to a church, connect with one. Look at the cross and be amazed that you get to be in a church in the presence of God. Then take a second look around you and say, "I'm with the people of God." Close your eyes and listen to them sing and wonder what one day it's going to be like in heaven when the angels are singing in the presence of God. That's the way you take your awe and increase it as the antidote.

And when you do that, I want you to remember these words from Paul to the Galatians: **"Let us not become weary in doing good"** (6:9). If apathy is not caring about the things God cares about, then when I have that

The response to apathy is action.

awe in mind, when the motivation is from the amazing love of God, then **"let us not become weary in doing good, for at the proper time we will reap a harvest if we do not give up."** There will be a harvest, a spiritual harvest! **"Therefore, as we have opportunity, let us do good to all people, especially those who belong to the family of believers"** (6:9,10).

When we know the antidote is awe, when our faith roots are stronger, when we're growing and going in the right direction and celebrating that every day, then here's the response to that apathy. God calls us to action to do good.

The response to apathy is action. Thinking about doing something isn't enough. God calls us to action.

So what is it that God would put on your heart that you need to do this week to act in your response to apathy? What's the action? What's the good thing you need to do? What's the thing you maybe haven't been caring about that you should care about, and what's the action step that you're going to take in the right direction? Will you set aside time for God's Word? Will you help someone in need? What step will you take?

God wants you and me to deal with apathy because he knows the destructive force it can be for us in this life and the deadly consequences it can have for our souls. My prayer is that we care about what God is passionate about and ask ourselves, "What good can I do today because I know he cares for me?"

Points to Ponder

Gather—Whether you gather in person or online with other Christians for worship, what one specific step will you take to deal with apathy in your life? Share your thoughts with a friend.

Group—Agree or Disagree: "Apathy feeds off of isolation." If you agree, in what ways have you experienced this when you haven't been together with other Christians? How has being with a group of other Christians helped you with apathy?

Grow—The Bible says, **"Consider him who endured such opposition from sinners, so that you will not grow weary and lose heart"** (Hebrews 12:3). Search the gospel accounts (Matthew, Mark, Luke, and John) to find a story from the life of Jesus when he endured opposition. What can you learn from that story?

Go—Do you know of any family member or friend who is apathetic in his or her relationship with Jesus? Reach out this week to that person and share with them what you appreciated from this chapter.

Prayer—Holy Spirit, instill in my heart the awe that I need to deal with apathy. Give me the light of knowing the goodness of God so that my life overflows with being good and kind and self-controlled. Help me be a person who acts after I think, knowing that the response to apathy is action. Help me carry out my mission and be passionate about the things you're passionate about. Amen.

Chapter 7
How to Deal With Death

This topic was saved for the last chapter for a reason. It's a difficult topic. It's hard for some people to read about, hard for some people to want to talk about or think about, and it might be hard for you for different reasons. Death might be something that's pretty raw. Maybe you're dealing with it right now. It might be something that a loved one went through recently, and you are still grieving. So it's still pretty difficult to address.

Some people haven't had to deal with death or haven't had a loved one die, but the subject is still very scary for them, and they don't like to think about it. Sometimes we like to keep death at a distance; we don't want to think about it. We put it out of our minds; we distract ourselves from it as much as we possibly can, until we can't. Then it's in our faces, and we have to deal with it.

I hate to be the one to tell you this, but you're not going to get out of this alive. You and I are going to die someday. There have been a lot of medical advancements. The lifespan of people has extended, yet the death rate has remained exactly the same; it's still 100 percent. We're not going to get out of this alive. If you don't live to an older age, you will be facing your own death. If you do live to an older age, not only will you face your own death, but you'll also have to deal with the death of many other people along the way. This is something we need to know how to do: How can we deal with death?

Now, you might want to wait until it's more real. Maybe wait until it's getting a little bit closer. The problem with that approach is you don't know how long you will be on this earth; that's problem number one. You don't know when your death will come or when somebody you love might die. You'll be unprepared.

The second reason you need to address it is that death is something that is extremely emotional. When it does happen, even when it's expected, it sends your emotions through the roof, keeping you from thinking logically. I can think of multiple occasions in my life when this happened because I've seen the death of loved ones more than once. But one in particular sticks out in my mind. When I was a missionary in Russia, I got a phone call late one afternoon and was told Ruslan, a 15-year-old boy who was a member of our church, ended his own life that afternoon. His sister and his mother were also members of our church. Nobody knew exactly what he was doing or what he was thinking; nobody knew these kinds of thoughts were going through his head. Ruslan went home and tied a rope around his neck. There were scratch marks on his neck; he was apparently trying to stop what he had started. Was he just goofing around, like teenage boys might do? Or was he really trying to end his life? We will never know; Ruslan died. And when I got that news, I went into my home office, closed the door, and cried. Then my emotions switched to anger. I was so mad at Ruslan. Why would he do that? It was so stupid and so permanent; why would he do that? Then I was back to crying again, and I was not thinking rationally for a little while until I could compose myself.

Maybe you've felt that way at the death of a loved one. People describe that kind of grief like suffocating. You can't breathe; there's this heavy weight on your chest. Some people describe it as brain fog; they can't think clearly, and people have to help them with some pretty basic tasks.

So we can't wait until it happens to learn how to deal

with it. It's something we need to do right now when we've got our wits about us. When our brains aren't foggy but they're clear, we need to talk about death.

As I was thinking about this topic and researching it, I thought, "I wonder what the world has to say about this topic of death?" If you take God out of the picture, if you forget about religion entirely, what would the world say? How does the world deal with this topic of death? Here's some of my research so you can learn what the world says when it comes to dealing with death.

We can't wait until it happens to learn how to deal with it.

Larry King was a famous journalist, and he did an interview back in 2015. He was already getting up there in years, and in that interview with *Times Magazine*, he said, "I can't get my head around one minute being there and another minute absent." Larry was not a Christian, and he and the world view death as a hard stop—here one minute and then nothing. He and the world believe that at death, we all cease to exist.

Of course, God tells us differently; there's something more after death. But don't our own consciences indicate that? It seems like even people who are agnostic or atheist, as they get up there in years and as death becomes more real, start to sense the same thing. It just doesn't feel right to think that this complex life, this intelligent life with all its experiences, is just gone and permanently ceases to exist. Yet that's what you're left with if you take God and religion completely out of the picture.

There was an ancient Greek philosopher named Epicurus who lived over three centuries before Christ. He had some theories about death. Here's what Epicurus said: "Death does not concern us because as long as we exist, death is not here. And when it does come, we no longer exist." That was his philosophy. There you go! Isn't that comforting? I guess we know how to deal with death, right? Clearly this worldly wisdom isn't overly helpful, is it?

I googled "How to deal with death?" and came across a podcast by that exact name by a couple of guys who like to take on edgy topics. Neither of them is Christian, and they had an entire one-hour podcast about how to deal with death. I listened with great interest, but I was gravely disappointed, which of course shouldn't have surprised me. The big takeaways I got from their podcast were not helpful. **Recognize your mortality; that was their first point.** You're not going to live forever; recognize it. Second, get comfortable with your mortality. Well, how do you do that? Talk about it at the dinner table, talk about it with your friends, and get more comfortable with the idea. And the third thing they said was you should prepare for your death, have a **living will, make sure your will and your affairs are in order so** that when you die things are in order. And that was about it. That podcast didn't make me feel any better. When it comes to dealing with death, worldly wisdom has nothing useful.

So let's look at God's wisdom. His wisdom is much more helpful. In fact, there is so much help for dealing with death **in the pages of the Bible that it was hard for me to figure out** what to focus on here. I could machine-gun a whole bunch of Bible passages that would give you comfort when you are dealing with death, but you won't remember them. So I decided to go to the exact opposite extreme. We're going to focus on one psalm—Psalm 16. But don't let this end here. Please continue to study this on your own. There's so much Scripture, so much comfort that God gives in his Word.

Let's work through Psalm 16. It was written by King David, a man who lived about three thousand years ago in

Palestine. He was very familiar with dealing with death. David himself was a soldier who was in countless battles. He ended the lives of a lot of people. His life was in danger countless times. There were other people who wanted to usurp his power and wanted to put him to death. On countless occasions, he almost died. He was probably in one of those situations, or thinking back on those situations, when he wrote this psalm.

Verse 1 starts like this: **"Keep me safe, my God, for in you I take refuge."** In other words, David knew that in an uncontrollable situation like when death is drawing near, there is only one place you can go, there's only one person whom you can flee to for refuge and safety. That is our God, who is the Lord of life and death; that's what David confesses in this psalm. **"Keep me safe, my God, for in you I take refuge. I say to the Lord, 'You are my Lord; apart from you I have no good thing'"** (verses 1,2). That sounds a little repetitious in English. But did you notice that the first *Lord* is in all caps and the second one isn't? It's because in Hebrew there are actually two different words here. Small caps Lord, is the great I am, the formal name God gave to himself. The name means he is absolute God who created all things, who never changes. He is the God of independent love whose love does not depend on us and our actions and our performance. Then David says that God is his Lord and his master who controls all things. David yields to God because he is God. David recognizes this and confesses this.

Then he says, **"Apart from you I have no good thing."** He knew that blessings could only come from the Lord. Next verses 3 and 4 say, **"I say of the holy people who are in the land, 'They are the noble ones in whom is all my delight.' Those who run after gods will suffer more and more. I will not pour out libations of blood to such gods** or take up their names on my lips."

There's one true God. And David says that he delights in the noble ones in the land. What David's saying is he delights in those who share his faith. He delights in those who believe in the Lord and who recognize that the Lord is the master. He delights in them and in walking with them. David recognizes that when you are dealing with life and death, surrounding yourself with—in his context, pagans; in our context, non-religious, non-churchgoing people—is not very helpful for you. I shared with you the worldly wisdom they might try to share with you, and it's not helpful. When things get toughest in life, it is so helpful, so delightful, to be surrounded by fellow believers who know the true God, who will share the true God with you, who will remind you of his counsel and his Word and his love and his wisdom and his protection and the safety that is in him and the provision that he gives. If we cut ourselves off from like-minded believers who know God like we know God, we'll miss a whole lot of comfort when we need it the very most.

Next David says, "Lord, **you alone are my portion and my cup**" (verse 5). We don't talk like that these days. But put it this way—the whole word is a smorgasbord. What portion will you take? What cup will you drink from? There are so many choices. David says, "The Lord is my portion. The Lord is my cup. He is the one who provides and satisfies. He's the one I would choose."

"You make my lot secure." *Lot* is like David's fate or future. The Lord makes it secure. Once again, the Lord is the Lord; he's the master. He's in control over all things. So, of course, in him David will be secure. He says, **"The boundary lines have fallen for me in pleasant places; surely I have a delightful inheritance"** (verse 6). You've got to put yourself in David's context. Back then, God's promises were also connected to the land God gave them. There are a lot of Old Testament laws related to making sure that land stayed within the family or clan. David makes this into a spiritual comparison or metaphor: "The boundary lines of my lot, of my property, have fallen in pleasant places. It's a pleasure to be here where you have put me, Lord. Surely I have a delightful inheritance. What I receive from you now and what I will receive from you later is awesome! God gives so much good."

Next David says, **"I will praise the Lord, who counsels me; even at night my heart instructs me"** (verse 7). David rejoices in the fact that he has the counsel of God. He has God speaking to him, and we do too. The Bible is the Word of God, the counsel of God. Read that book and find out the principles and promises of God that give you so much joy, that guide you in life, that tell you what's to come after life. David says, **"Even at night my heart instructs me."** In other words, "It's dark; I can't open my Bible and read it, but my heart instructs me because I've been meditating on that Word. I have that Word packed into my mind and into my heart so that's what I think about." Has that ever happened to you? You wake up in the middle of the night, your mind starts racing, and for me, it's often about the troubles or the things I'm concerned about or stressed about. And David says, "Yeah, me too. I sometimes wake up in the night too, but my heart instructs me." He remembers the promises of God and the protection and safety of God because that Word is so much in him because he has studied it that much.

Now here is a key verse: **"I keep my eyes always on the Lord. With him at my right hand, I will not be shaken"** (verse 8). There are so many other things we keep at our right hand; there are so many other things that we sinful human beings draw near and rely upon instead of God.

Maybe it's money. If my bank account gets big enough, if my retirement account is fat enough, then no matter what happens in my life—with my money at my right hand—I will be able to handle it. David would tell you, "No, you're wrong." If you're relying on money, if that's what's at your right hand, you will be shaken someday.

If at your right hand the thing you rely upon the most is another human being, even if it's your spouse, and that is where you find all your peace and hope and rest, then someday you will be shaken because either you or your spouse will die. If you are holding close your career, your intelligence, your skill, your ability and that's what you rely upon because you are so capable, you're going to be shaken because someday those things aren't going to get you through anymore. If for comfort and peace when you feel stressed out you turn to alcohol, drugs, or some other form of addiction, I promise you this, sooner or later, you will be shaken.

You will not be shaken with the Lord at your right hand.

But David knows better. He says, "With the Lord at my right hand, I will not be shaken." Even when you have to deal with death, you will not be shaken with the Lord at your right hand.

"Therefore my heart is glad and my tongue rejoices." Even if you're dealing with death? Yes, even then, because you look to the Lord and trust in him. David says, **"My body also will rest secure because you will not abandon me to the realm of the dead, nor will you let your faithful one see decay"** (verses 9,10). David had a belief in the afterlife. David knew what the people of this world do not: Death is not a ceasing to exist, and there is a life after death. It does go on, and David had full confidence as he thought about that life that was to come.

Now there's an interesting part of this psalm that we need to unpack just a little bit more. He said that "you will not let your faithful one see decay." David believed in the resurrection, but did he really think that his body wouldn't decay? Well, if he did, he was wrong because it did.

For insight on this verse, look to the New Testament. In Acts chapter 2, the apostle Peter preached a sermon in which he quoted Psalm 16 and gave us some insight into what David was thinking. Before a crowd of thousands of people, about ten days after Jesus had ascended back into heaven, filled with the Holy Spirit preaching to this crowd, Peter told them all about Jesus, how he was God's own Son and how he was crucified on a cross because of sinful men. But on the third day, he rose from the dead. Then Peter went on to prove this resurrection of Jesus from the dead was, first of all, foretold by Jesus himself, but the prophets of the Old Testament also prophesied about it, and then Jesus did it. That's what Peter said in Acts chapter 2: **"Fellow Israelites, I can tell you confidently that the patriarch David died and was buried, and his tomb is here to this day. But he was a prophet and he knew that God had promised him an oath that he would place one of his descendants on his throne"** (verses 29,30). David knew God's promise that there would be a descendant of David who would become a king who would rule over everything and whose kingdom would have no end. The kingdom would be eternal and go on and on and on. David knew that because God had promised that to him.

So David, seeing what was to come, speaks of the res- urrection of the Messiah; that's what he's talking about in those verses that we just looked at. He is talking about the resurrection of the Messiah, that he was not abandoned to the realm of the dead, nor did his body see decay. **"God has raised this Jesus to life, and we are all witnesses of it,"**

Peter said (Acts 2:32). David, in speaking the words of Psalm 16:10, was a prophet. He saw with prophetic vision that a thousand years later, one of his descendants, Jesus, who was of the line of David, would live, die, and rise on the third day before his body saw any decay. David knew that, because of the coming Messiah and King who would reign forever, his body would not remain in the grave either. David knew he would live even though he died. That was David's confidence, and it's ours too.

Then the final verse of the psalm says this: **"You make known to me the path of life; you will fill me with joy in your presence, with eternal pleasures at your right hand"** (verse 11). David had this eager anticipation of the life to come because he knew he would be in God's immediate presence and there would be no more mourning or suffering or pain or sorrow or death and that he would live forever. David celebrated the fact that the Lord had made known to him this path of life. And the good news is this: God has made known to you this path of life as well.

What is this path of life? Jesus couldn't have said it any more clearly himself when in John 14:6, he said this: **"I am the way,"** the path, **"the truth and the life. No one comes to the Father except through me."** Jesus is that path of life because the wages of sin is death. Jesus, God's own Son, took on human flesh, lived among us, was perfect, blameless, holy, true. No sin! So what should have happened to Jesus? Life! But what did Jesus do? He said, "I'm taking your sin from you and putting it on me. I am responsible; you are not." Because Jesus has taken your sin, what does Jesus have to do? He has to go to that cross, and he has to die, and that's exactly what he did in his love for you.

> God has made known to you this path of life as well.

And as David said, on the third day, he rose from the dead, he conquered sin, he conquered death, and that means all who are in Christ Jesus have this gift of eternal life. That is God's gift to you in Christ Jesus. This is the path of life, which David believed. This is the path of life for you.

Wow, there's a lot in that psalm! So much to enjoy that I would encourage you to keep coming back to it. You will be so happy as you celebrate what God has given you and what God has done for you.

Just to summarize quickly, there are seven things this psalm shows us about God that we can celebrate and rejoice.

1. God is Lord. He is the one in control. He is the one who created all things. He's the one who holds you in his hands. You will have great comfort when you are dealing with death if you remember that God is Lord.

2. God gives refuge. He is unmovable and solid. Flee to him for safety. You will not be shaken with God at your right hand. You are not alone; he is with you. You have confidence and will not be shaken no matter what you go through in this world.

3. God gives counsel. His Word is there for you. He speaks to you in the pages of Scripture. Treasure the counsel of God and celebrate the fact that God reveals things in his Word.

4. God gives community. When you are part of a church community, they are like-minded people who are looking to the Lord and celebrating the safety that is in him. When you are dealing with something as difficult as death, these are the people who are going to walk with you through it and remind you of the love of God and his safety and the provision that he gives in Christ Jesus.

5. God gives pleasure. Even in this broken world, we enjoy some pleasure. But in his eternal presence, the floodgates will open, unlimited all the time. Pleasure is what God promises. No matter what your circumstances, even when facing death, you can have joy because you know that there is a much better life to come.

6. God provides. He provides for everything we need for body and soul. You are provided for in this world, and the retirement plan of God is out of this world. The inheritance that he promises you—the kingdom of God—belongs to you.

7. God gives life—eternal life in Christ Jesus as a gift. It's yours through God. You have the very presence of God now and forever.

I want you to remember this: Keep your eyes always on the Lord. No matter what you're going through in life, or if you're at the end of life, keep your eyes on the Lord.

Points to Ponder

Gather—Those who are grieving the loss of a loved one often withdraw and isolate themselves. Romans 12:15 says, **"Mourn with those who mourn."** Do you agree that gathering together with other Christians in worship is like oxygen to someone suffering with grief? Why or why not? Do you know of anyone who can barely breathe?

Group—There are organizations and ministries that support people who are grieving the loss of a loved one. One is GriefShare (www.griefshare.org). If you are grieving or know someone who is, check out their website for resources and support.

Grow—How do the following verses comfort one dealing with death? Discuss each verse with another person. Do you know of any other verses in the Bible to add to this list?

- John 3:16
- 1 Thessalonians 4:14
- John 11:25,26
- Romans 6:23
- Psalm 23:4
- Revelation 21:4
- Romans 14:8
- Luke 23:43
- John 14:1-6

Go—When a person is dealing with death, the door for sharing the good news of Jesus is often open the widest. You have the Word of our God that gives hope! Watch for opportunities, and boldly share it with those who need comfort.

Prayer—Dear heavenly Father, we struggle in this world with so many different things, and probably the hardest one is death. Whether it's the death of a loved one or when we're facing our own death, it's extraordinarily difficult. And yet, unlike this world, you give us so much comfort. We know that we've got you and with you we do not need to be afraid. We know that you provide safety, that you give good counsel, that you give all we need, and that you have made known to us the path of life. So with you, Lord, at our side, we will not be shaken. So help us, Lord, always keep our eyes only on you. Amen.

Conclusion

The authors of this book are not providing a conclusion. Instead, they are asking you to be the conclusion by journaling your thoughts.

We suggest you jot down your takeaways from each of the seven chapters:

- What did you learn from the Bible teachings?

- What thoughts filled your heart and mind as you turned each page?

- Which of the seven chapters were the most meaningful or helpful to you?

- By having read this book, what difference will it make in your relationship to God, with others, and with yourself?

How to deal with *ME*? Open the Bible and start reading. You will experience his blessing!

About Time of Grace

Time of Grace is an independent, donor-funded ministry that connects people to God's grace—his love, glory, and power—so they realize the temporary things of life don't satisfy. What brings satisfaction is knowing that because Jesus lived, died, and rose for all of us, we have access to the eternal God—right now and forever.

To discover more, please visit timeofgrace.org or call 800.661.3311.

Help share God's message of grace!

Every gift you give helps Time of Grace reach people around the world with the good news of Jesus. Your generosity and prayer support take the gospel of grace to others through our ministry outreach and help them experience a satisfied life as they see God all around them.

Give today at timeofgrace.org/give or by calling 800.661.3311.

Thank you!

About 922 Ministries

I have become all things to all people
so that by all possible means I might save some.
(1 Corinthians 9:22)

The apostle Paul wrote those words two thousand years ago. They still speak to the purpose of the church . . . to share Jesus with others even if it means sacrificing our personal preferences. We strive "to become all things to all people" without compromising God's truth or grace so that lives might be transformed for now and for eternity. That's what 1 Corinthians 9:22 ministry looks like no matter what time in history it is.

922 Ministries is a Lutheran Christian organization that consists of multiple campuses in the Fox Valley Area of Wisconsin. St. Peter Lutheran Church and The CORE seek to reach everyone who is impacted by the world's changing culture with the changeless gospel, by using traditional and innovative ministries. The also partner with Time of Grace Ministry to reach people globally.